# GET THE LIFE YOU L♡VE
## and live it

Transform your life in just 12 weeks
with daily power actions

## Arvind Devalia

## DEDICATION

This book is dedicated to the memory of my dear mother and my middle brother who both passed away in 2022.

They have been there for me always and have guided me to revise my original book.

I dedicate the rest of my life to honour the memory of both my late parents and my brother - and live my best life. They would want me to thrive, prosper, and be happy.

I know they are always with me, guiding me and looking out for my growth and wellbeing.

I invite you to also live your life in such a way so as to honour your loved ones.

# CONTENTS

How to Use this Book . . . . . . . . . . . . . . . . . . . . . . . . . . . . . . . . . . . . 1

Introduction –
Time to Follow Your Childhood Dreams. . . . . . . . . . . . . . . . . . . . . . . 2

  1.  Adopt an Attitude of Gratitude . . . . . . . . . . . . . . . . . . . . . . . 4

  2.  Create an Inspiring Vision for Your Life . . . . . . . . . . . . . . . . 8

  3.  Clarify Your Core Life Values . . . . . . . . . . . . . . . . . . . . . . . 12

  4.  Find Your Life Purpose . . . . . . . . . . . . . . . . . . . . . . . . . . . . 16

  5.  Set Inspiring Life Goals . . . . . . . . . . . . . . . . . . . . . . . . . . . 20

  6.  Clear All the Clutter from Your Life . . . . . . . . . . . . . . . . . 24

  7.  Build Up Your Self-Esteem . . . . . . . . . . . . . . . . . . . . . . . . . 28

  8.  Appreciate All the Abundance Around You. . . . . . . . . . . . . . 32

  9.  Give and Receive Openly. . . . . . . . . . . . . . . . . . . . . . . . . . . 36

10.  Be Positive and Joyous Everyday . . . . . . . . . . . . . . . . . . . . 40

11.  Become Self-Confident and Fearless . . . . . . . . . . . . . . . . . . 44

12.  Keep Your Cool and Become Peaceful . . . . . . . . . . . . . . . . . 48

13.  Strive for Excellence Always . . . . . . . . . . . . . . . . . . . . . . . . 52

14.  Get into Action Now. . . . . . . . . . . . . . . . . . . . . . . . . . . . . . 56

15.  Enjoy the Work You Do Now . . . . . . . . . . . . . . . . . . . . . . . 60

16.  Find the Work you Love. . . . . . . . . . . . . . . . . . . . . . . . . . . . 64

17.  Create Work-Life Balance . . . . . . . . . . . . . . . . . . . . . . . . . 68

18.  Manage Your Money. . . . . . . . . . . . . . . . . . . . . . . . . . . . . . 72

19.  Take Total Self-Care . . . . . . . . . . . . . . . . . . . . . . . . . . . . . . 76

20.  Increase Your Energy and Zest for Life. . . . . . . . . . . . . . . . . 80

21.  Improve All Your Relationships . . . . . . . . . . . . . . . . . . . . . 84

22.  Enjoy Your Single Life . . . . . . . . . . . . . . . . . . . . . . . . . . . . 88

23.  Create Your Dream Relationship . . . . . . . . . . . . . . . . . . . . 92

24.  Transform your Existing Love Relationship . . . . . . . . . . . . . . . . . . . 96

25.  Create Sunshine All Year-Round in Your Life. . . . . . . . . . . . . . . . . 100

Final Words from Arvind – Make Your Life Count. . . . . . . . . . . . . . . . 104

Words of Inspiration . . . . . . . . . . . . . . . . . . . . . . . . . . . . . . . . . . . . 106

Inspiring Quotations . . . . . . . . . . . . . . . . . . . . . . . . . . . . . . . . . . . . 114

Notes. . . . . . . . . . . . . . . . . . . . . . . . . . . . . . . . . . . . . . . . . . . . . . . . 116

Recommended Books . . . . . . . . . . . . . . . . . . . . . . . . . . . . . . . . . . . 119

With Deep Gratitude . . . . . . . . . . . . . . . . . . . . . . . . . . . . . . . . . . . . 120

Further Key Resources . . . . . . . . . . . . . . . . . . . . . . . . . . . . . . . . . . . 121

About the Author . . . . . . . . . . . . . . . . . . . . . . . . . . . . . . . . . . . . . . . 122

# HOW TO USE THIS BOOK

This book comprises of 25 separate chapters.

Each chapter covers a different and important part of your life – and each chapter has key power actions to transform that area of your life. As you take action and focus on making incremental changes, you can begin to transform your life.

You should ideally go through the chapters in the sequence they are presented, but feel free to browse and get a flavour of what is to come. You may also choose to skip a few chapters as you feel appropriate, returning to review them later.

For instance, if you are stressed out and you want to improve your work-life balance, you might want to go straight to step 17, which is all about obtaining work-life balance.

Take a brief look at the contents pages to see what these chapters are. Then you can get started immediately. This is an action-orientated book, so read and reflect on the questions I pose at the end of each chapter.

Go through all the chapters and carry out the actions within 12 weeks, and your life will be transformed in just 12 weeks.

**You must be prepared to put in some effort to ultimately create the life you want and deserve.**

As you go through the book, make sure you have a pen or pencil with you. When you get to the power action pages at the end of each chapter, be prepared to write down whatever comes to your mind.

By writing these things down, you become clearer about your insights, plans and ideas. There are no right or wrong answers, just self-learning, and appreciation of yourself.

I have included a few blank pages at the back for you to write additional notes. At the back of the book, you will also find several inspirational verses and quotations, which I hope you find as inspiring and motivating as I have.

Life is meant to be full of ease, grace, and joy, and in the same way, this book is simple to use, clear and fun. I sincerely hope that you will go through all the chapters and carry out the power actions. You will then be well on your way to creating the life you love.

**Enjoy this journey – your life will never be the same again.**

**You are about to transform your life in just 12 weeks...**

# INTRODUCTION

## TIME TO FOLLOW YOUR CHILDHOOD DREAMS

The book you are about to dive into is the result of many hundreds of hours of work with people around the world. It will help you create the life you love – and live it.

This book is about living a life with purpose, commitment and making a difference to yourself and others in whatever way works for you.

It's about having great relationships, vibrant health and fulfilling work. It is also about growing your self-awareness and achieving your goals – whether they are to make more money, find your life partner, express your creativity or becoming healthy and fit. Or maybe you want to go out there and make a huge difference in the world.

**I offer you simple, tried, and tested ways of creating and living the life you love.**

I take you through 25 short chapters using my own life story as the backdrop. I want to help you get the life you love through the lessons I have learnt and by sharing some key insights and many simple tips I have picked up along the way.

Everyone's life is a journey of growth and learning. By integrating my own story, I hope that you too can relate to your own life and see what you can do to create your life the way you want it to be. Of course, my life is an evolving story and there is so much more I want to be, do, and have. It is an exciting journey and I want you to feel the same way about your life.

For many years, I had this restless feeling that I had not yet accomplished enough. Yet by most people's standards, I was quite successful. I seemed to have it all – a great job, lovely home, happy marriage, financial security. But I now know that just wasn't enough – nor was all as it seemed on the outside. Inside, I was not happy, or content and I was rather frustrated - this led to stress and ill health. Part of this frustration was that I felt I had been 'given' a lot and I therefore expected a lot of myself.

Having been a very academic child and having achieved exceptional exam results, I also carried with me high expectations from my parents, siblings, and friends, which led me to often have the sense that I was underachieving. I gradually let go of this sense of underachieving by focusing on all the things that I actually managed to do rather than on the 'did nots' – and by taking steps to realize my potential in a new way.

In the same way, you too can start today from exactly where you are. Reading this book is just the beginning – you can now begin to create and live the life you were always meant to.

Whatever life throws at you, going through these 25 chapters will help you build a firm foundation for your life. Never underestimate the profound resiliency of your human spirit, or how swiftly things can change for the better – often overnight.

To start with, become aware of the magic happening all around you. Look for the magic in the moment. For example, as I write this in my garden, I can see bees hopping around from flower to flower, continuing their natural cycle from millions of years ago.

Every bee and every flower matters. Together they are part of this wonderful tapestry we call life. Nature just takes its course, and you are just as important a part of all this amazing magic happening around us. You matter too.

**Always remember that you matter.**

I have also had the awareness that I have been holding myself back all my life in the presence of other people. I was always self-effacing and could not take a compliment.

For me this was partly a cultural thing as I come from an Indian background, and I have been brought up to be humble and quiet. But more importantly it was due to this fear of failure and of looking stupid. Like a lot of people, I was my own worst critic and a non-forgiving censor of my words before they had even left my mouth.

It wasn't always like this – I remember being a very confident child at one point. As I grew older, I seemed to sabotage my own success and ended up doing 'average' in my university exams – average by my own high standards. I performed 'average' in a series of jobs and never really excelled in my early careers – first in IT and then in Marketing.

As I went from one job to another, the feeling grew stronger that I ought to be doing something else. I kept remembering that as a child I wanted to change the world by ending poverty and bringing about world peace. I even wanted to win the Nobel peace prize! But like a lot of people somewhere along the way, I gave up on such dreams and began living a 'normal' life.

I remember in my first year at university, I told my friends I wanted to go to India and help the people there improve their lives. I got some sceptical looks and was told that everyone wanted to do such things and it was all just fancy talk. I did finally do just that – I went to India and served at a charity school, with which I remain very involved to this day – though it took me almost twenty years to get there!

When I finally visited Nirvana school in South India, I regretted not having gone much earlier to India and fulfilling my university pledge, but I now know that I had to go through the intervening years to get there. My life lessons and experiences during the many years helped me to contribute and make a difference in exactly the way I had envisioned all those years ago.

**As I write this, I wonder what childhood dreams you have given up on.**

When will you begin to make them come true?

For me, visiting Nirvana school transformed my life deeply in many ways, and ultimately led me to become a coach and to write this book. I feel there are many more good things yet to come as this is just the beginning of the next stage of my journey.

**In the same way, your life too is an evolving story and there is so much more you can be, do and have.**

It is an exciting journey and I want you to feel excited about the journey you are about to undertake.

I sincerely hope that as you continue your own life journey, through this book I can encourage, support, and inspire you to also get the life you love – and live it.

**Let's begin.**

# 1 - ADOPT AN ATTITUDE OF GRATITUDE

To create a life you love, it is vital to adopt an attitude of gratitude. It all begins with cultivating and nurturing a mindset of gratitude.

Are you grateful for your life? Do you see your glass as half full or half empty?

Gratitude is all about appreciating the things you have in your life. It is a way of reaching back to your natural state of happiness. You get to notice what's right instead of what's wrong, and you begin to see every 'problem' as an opportunity for growth and development. Have you noticed the happiest people in the world always seem to live with an attitude of gratitude.

Sometimes I am so full of appreciation for this life – my gifts and my blessings, that I am simply overcome with gratitude. At such moments, I could cry and all of life seems so worthwhile. All challenges, past and present just fade away in such moments.

An example of this is when a lovely new friend once arrived at my home for dinner, literally laden with gifts of flowers, food, a lotus plant for my home and a thank you card – it was all just so beautiful, considerate, and overwhelming – I cried tears of joy and appreciation. And I seek more such moments.

**Remember that there are no 'ordinary' moments.**

I once wrote a list of 100 things I am grateful for, and I continue to add to this list since I found it to be quite a powerful exercise. Are you aware of all the goodness around you? The fact that you are breathing and reading these printed words is a marvel in itself. Have you noticed, so often we take something for granted and then miss it as soon as it has gone.

Many a time a loved one has left us, only for us to wish we had told them just how much they meant to us. In 2022, I lost both my brother and my mother within 5 months of each other, and though I am deeply grateful for all our wonderful moments together, I still wish I had told them more often just how much I loved them and just what they meant to me.

Begin this week to value all the goodness and beauty around you. This can be as majestic as a sunset or as simple as the feel of the clothes you wear. Be thankful for a gift from a friend, a child's smile, a stranger's kindness, having got home safely yesterday and simply to be alive.

We often complain about the weather being too hot, too cold, too wet, too dry, but everything has a reason. We need the rain to sustain growth so instead of complaining it has spoilt our plans for a picnic we can instead appreciate it as the force that has helped plants, fruit and vegetables grow.

Just get present to the beauty and majesty of a sunset as you sit and watch the sun go down and at the same time, be in awe of the sheer power and force of nature as seen in thunderous rainstorms.

List the things in your life to be grateful for, which you may be taking for granted. This could include your health, home, family, friends, work colleagues, or your car. Add all the things that you could not survive without, such as sunlight, air, water, and food. For now, begin to reflect on these, and at the end of this section you will get a chance to write them down.

Focus on what is right in your life rather than what is wrong. Count your blessings and be thankful. Do something for someone, for no reason other than simply wanting to do it. Have no attachment to the outcome. Pay for someone's parking or compliment a stranger.

Post a card of appreciation to someone whom you have not been in touch with for a while. Go one step further and send cards to five people and tell them how much you appreciate them being in your life. Send a thank you note to someone who has done something for you, significant or not. Get into a habit of sending such notes by post. Create a trail of happiness behind you, as you go forward in your life.

Accept things as they are. No matter how much a situation has turned out to be very different from your expectations, accept that it is the way it is. You don't know how much worse off you could have been, had things gone differently. Savour the current moment and be grateful.

Gifts come to us in all shapes and sizes every minute of the day, if only we can become open to acknowledging and receiving them. Every incident and interaction with another human being contains a gift for our learning and growth. Trust that all is well and that things are evolving in perfect harmony.

**Take time to feel awe and wonder at the world. See things as if for the first time ever. Slow down and notice the beauty around you. Stop and use all your senses.**

For many years now, I have been spending a lot of time in Regents Park, London, near my home. It has a fantastic rose garden that nowadays seems to be in flower eight months of the year, full of roses that look and smell beautiful, yet prickly to touch. This has become a haven for me – see if you can find your own haven, whether that is a garden, somewhere near water, in a quiet corner of an art gallery. Experiment and find whatever that works for you.

Say 'thank you' as often as possible to all the people who make your life what it is. Make a game of it – count the number of times you can say thank you each day. Observe how all the people you acknowledge seem truly touched.

As you create the life you love, always remember that your life is brimming over with goodness. And through your gratitude will come many more gifts which will allow you to be truly the best you can be, both for yourself and for all those around you.

**From today onwards, adopt an attitude of gratitude as a life-long commitment.**

# Power Actions to Adopt an Attitude of Gratitude

Write down 10 things that you are grateful for in your life.

1. . . . . . . . . . . . . . . . . . . . . . . . . . . . . . . . . . . . . . . . . . . . . . . . .

2. . . . . . . . . . . . . . . . . . . . . . . . . . . . . . . . . . . . . . . . . . . . . . . . .

3. . . . . . . . . . . . . . . . . . . . . . . . . . . . . . . . . . . . . . . . . . . . . . . . .

4. . . . . . . . . . . . . . . . . . . . . . . . . . . . . . . . . . . . . . . . . . . . . . . . .

5. . . . . . . . . . . . . . . . . . . . . . . . . . . . . . . . . . . . . . . . . . . . . . . . .

6. . . . . . . . . . . . . . . . . . . . . . . . . . . . . . . . . . . . . . . . . . . . . . . . .

7. . . . . . . . . . . . . . . . . . . . . . . . . . . . . . . . . . . . . . . . . . . . . . . . .

8. . . . . . . . . . . . . . . . . . . . . . . . . . . . . . . . . . . . . . . . . . . . . . . . .

9. . . . . . . . . . . . . . . . . . . . . . . . . . . . . . . . . . . . . . . . . . . . . . . . .

10. . . . . . . . . . . . . . . . . . . . . . . . . . . . . . . . . . . . . . . . . . . . . . . . .

Choose three of the most important people in your life. Tell them today, what you love and appreciate most about them.

1. . . . . . . . . . . . . . . . . . . . . . . . . . . . . . . . . . . . . . . . . . . . . . . . .

. . . . . . . . . . . . . . . . . . . . . . . . . . . . . . . . . . . . . . . . . . . . . . . .

. . . . . . . . . . . . . . . . . . . . . . . . . . . . . . . . . . . . . . . . . . . . . . . .

2. . . . . . . . . . . . . . . . . . . . . . . . . . . . . . . . . . . . . . . . . . . . . . . . .

. . . . . . . . . . . . . . . . . . . . . . . . . . . . . . . . . . . . . . . . . . . . . . . .

. . . . . . . . . . . . . . . . . . . . . . . . . . . . . . . . . . . . . . . . . . . . . . . .

3. . . . . . . . . . . . . . . . . . . . . . . . . . . . . . . . . . . . . . . . . . . . . . . . .

. . . . . . . . . . . . . . . . . . . . . . . . . . . . . . . . . . . . . . . . . . . . . . . .

. . . . . . . . . . . . . . . . . . . . . . . . . . . . . . . . . . . . . . . . . . . . . . . .

List up to 10 other people to whom you will show your appreciation this week. How will you show your appreciation in the next seven days?

1. . . . . . . . . . . . . . . . . . . . . . . . . . . . . . . . . . . . . . . . . . . . . . . . . . . . . .

2. . . . . . . . . . . . . . . . . . . . . . . . . . . . . . . . . . . . . . . . . . . . . . . . . . . . . .

3. . . . . . . . . . . . . . . . . . . . . . . . . . . . . . . . . . . . . . . . . . . . . . . . . . . . . .

4. . . . . . . . . . . . . . . . . . . . . . . . . . . . . . . . . . . . . . . . . . . . . . . . . . . . . .

5. . . . . . . . . . . . . . . . . . . . . . . . . . . . . . . . . . . . . . . . . . . . . . . . . . . . . .

6. . . . . . . . . . . . . . . . . . . . . . . . . . . . . . . . . . . . . . . . . . . . . . . . . . . . . .

7. . . . . . . . . . . . . . . . . . . . . . . . . . . . . . . . . . . . . . . . . . . . . . . . . . . . . .

8. . . . . . . . . . . . . . . . . . . . . . . . . . . . . . . . . . . . . . . . . . . . . . . . . . . . . .

9. . . . . . . . . . . . . . . . . . . . . . . . . . . . . . . . . . . . . . . . . . . . . . . . . . . . . .

10. . . . . . . . . . . . . . . . . . . . . . . . . . . . . . . . . . . . . . . . . . . . . . . . . . . . .

Describe five ways that you will use every day, to show your appreciation of the goodness around you. *For example, saying thank you often, taking walks in nature, sending notes of appreciation to your loved ones.*

1. . . . . . . . . . . . . . . . . . . . . . . . . . . . . . . . . . . . . . . . . . . . . . . . . . . . . .

   . . . . . . . . . . . . . . . . . . . . . . . . . . . . . . . . . . . . . . . . . . . . . . . . . . . . .

2. . . . . . . . . . . . . . . . . . . . . . . . . . . . . . . . . . . . . . . . . . . . . . . . . . . . . .

   . . . . . . . . . . . . . . . . . . . . . . . . . . . . . . . . . . . . . . . . . . . . . . . . . . . . .

3. . . . . . . . . . . . . . . . . . . . . . . . . . . . . . . . . . . . . . . . . . . . . . . . . . . . . .

   . . . . . . . . . . . . . . . . . . . . . . . . . . . . . . . . . . . . . . . . . . . . . . . . . . . . .

4. . . . . . . . . . . . . . . . . . . . . . . . . . . . . . . . . . . . . . . . . . . . . . . . . . . . . .

   . . . . . . . . . . . . . . . . . . . . . . . . . . . . . . . . . . . . . . . . . . . . . . . . . . . . .

5. . . . . . . . . . . . . . . . . . . . . . . . . . . . . . . . . . . . . . . . . . . . . . . . . . . . . .

   . . . . . . . . . . . . . . . . . . . . . . . . . . . . . . . . . . . . . . . . . . . . . . . . . . . . .

## 2 – CREATE AN INSPIRING VISION FOR YOUR LIFE

**B**efore you start creating the life you love, you must know what you wish to create. As you begin to create a life you love, just what is the vision of your life?

Do you love the life you have? If you had a chance to start afresh today, what would you do differently? Since every new day is also the first day of the rest of your life, ask yourself what you can do today, to help you create the life you desire, and indeed the life you deserve.

I feel that my life now is the best it has ever been, and I know that there is much more goodness to come. The underlying vision for my life in recent years has been one of service to others in every way I can. As I continue to do what I do and love, my vision becomes clearer and even bigger, and my life seems to work even better as time goes by.

What I do is serve and support people to improve their lives in several ways. Firstly, I am a transformational coach, enabling individuals and companies to excel. I back this up through my writing, workshops and speaking events. I support a few charitable organisations through fund-raising, awareness building and hands on assistance. I also hold numerous events whereby people can come together as a community so as to connect and support each other for mutual growth, benefit, and friendship.

A clear vision for your life is simply a picture of your future that you create with your imagination. This vision becomes a guiding image of accomplishment and fulfilment for you, and others. Seeing in detail what you want in your future allows you to go all out and make more of what you want possible.

- **What really excites you?**
- **What are you passionate about?**
- **What contribution do you want to make to the world?**
- **What do you want to be remembered for?**
- **What unique talents do you have to offer the world?**

A very important part of this exercise is also to ask yourself what it's costing you right now for not pursuing your vision. The cost to you could be stress, ill health, and general dissatisfaction with your life.

Spend some quiet time on your own, think about the rest of your life and ask yourself just what you would like to have achieved? Focus on those things you want to have done in your life before it is over. It might be to visit a place, a bungee jump, see all five continents, learn to drive and so on. For now, simply begin to think about these and after reading the rest of this section you will find space on the next page to write down your thoughts.

Allow your imagination to run riot thinking about the things you want to have done ranging from the ordinary to the most daring adventures. Personally, I visited the Grand Canyon twenty years ago and would love to go back but this time I would like to take a helicopter ride and also trek down to the bottom of the canyon with some friendly mules.

Knowing what you dislike, or don't want in your life, will help you clarify what you do want instead. For example, if you don't like renting, you could instead decide to work towards owning your own home. Or if you resent working for someone else you could look at starting your own business.

I really resented working in a bank and I eventually began looking for alternate opportunities. Things always work out for the best – I was made redundant the same week as I got accepted for my MBA course at Business School!

We can learn so much from ordinary people doing some extraordinary things, such as the athletes who compete in the Paralympic Games. We might also consider figureheads such as Mahatma Gandhi, who dedicated his whole life to an independent India free from British rule and Nelson Mandela who stood by his commitment to a united and integrated South Africa despite being locked up for 27 years. They can inspire us to reach for the highest levels.

Become open to new ideas. As you reflect on your vision, grab all the ideas and experiences that come your way. Always carry a notepad with you and write down every idea that shows up in your life, no matter how strange it may seem to you. As you reflect and write, do not listen to your inner voice which may begin to censor, criticise, or judge your thoughts.

Project yourself into the future 20 years from now, or whatever time-period appeals to you, and imagine looking back on your life.

- **What accomplishments do you want to look back on with pride?**
- **What would you need to have done, for you to feel that you have had a full life and that you have lived to your full potential?**
- **Will you have maximised all your talents?**

I once worked with a remarkable American woman who told me that she had done just this exercise 20 years before when she had been a teenager – and she had already accomplished more than many people do in a lifetime. She had seen most of the world, had financial freedom, played in a musical band, owned her own recording studio, and bred Siamese cats. She was also a top computer consultant and had studied the law and medicine. She had no regrets about her life and was focused on doing all the remaining things she had always wanted to.

Ask what you would want people around you such as family, friends, or work colleagues to say about the life that you have lived. What contribution to them and to society generally, would you want to be remembered for? Just how great a difference do you want to have made in their lives?

Reconnect with your original strengths and passions; reflect on who you were before the demands of daily life transformed you into someone else. The expectations of those people around you such as parents, teachers, peers, work colleagues may well have made you lose your original self. Get in touch once again with how you were as a child and remember if there were any special roles or games that you enjoyed playing most.

Ask yourself if it became necessary to make your vision come true, would you be open and willing to make short term financial sacrifices, along with tough and painful personal decisions. Similarly, if it came to it, consider if you would be prepared to let go of current attachments and comforts. Consider what you would do, if you had all the time and money in the world and knew you could not fail at whatever you attempted.

How would you feel if asked this question in the years to come:

**What do you wish you had done in your life?**

## Power Actions to Create an Inspiring Vision for Your Life

Spend some quiet time on your own. Visualise the things you want to do, in great detail. Get excited about your future. Write out a list of 20 things you want to do in your lifetime.

1. . . . . . . . . . . . . . . . . . . . . . . . . . . . . . . . . . . . . . . . . . . . . . . . .

2. . . . . . . . . . . . . . . . . . . . . . . . . . . . . . . . . . . . . . . . . . . . . . . . .

3. . . . . . . . . . . . . . . . . . . . . . . . . . . . . . . . . . . . . . . . . . . . . . . . .

4. . . . . . . . . . . . . . . . . . . . . . . . . . . . . . . . . . . . . . . . . . . . . . . . .

5. . . . . . . . . . . . . . . . . . . . . . . . . . . . . . . . . . . . . . . . . . . . . . . . .

6. . . . . . . . . . . . . . . . . . . . . . . . . . . . . . . . . . . . . . . . . . . . . . . . .

7. . . . . . . . . . . . . . . . . . . . . . . . . . . . . . . . . . . . . . . . . . . . . . . . .

8. . . . . . . . . . . . . . . . . . . . . . . . . . . . . . . . . . . . . . . . . . . . . . . . .

9. . . . . . . . . . . . . . . . . . . . . . . . . . . . . . . . . . . . . . . . . . . . . . . . .

10. . . . . . . . . . . . . . . . . . . . . . . . . . . . . . . . . . . . . . . . . . . . . . . . .

11. . . . . . . . . . . . . . . . . . . . . . . . . . . . . . . . . . . . . . . . . . . . . . . . .

12. . . . . . . . . . . . . . . . . . . . . . . . . . . . . . . . . . . . . . . . . . . . . . . . .

13. . . . . . . . . . . . . . . . . . . . . . . . . . . . . . . . . . . . . . . . . . . . . . . . .

14. . . . . . . . . . . . . . . . . . . . . . . . . . . . . . . . . . . . . . . . . . . . . . . . .

15. . . . . . . . . . . . . . . . . . . . . . . . . . . . . . . . . . . . . . . . . . . . . . . . .

16. . . . . . . . . . . . . . . . . . . . . . . . . . . . . . . . . . . . . . . . . . . . . . . . .

17. . . . . . . . . . . . . . . . . . . . . . . . . . . . . . . . . . . . . . . . . . . . . . . . .

18. . . . . . . . . . . . . . . . . . . . . . . . . . . . . . . . . . . . . . . . . . . . . . . . .

19. . . . . . . . . . . . . . . . . . . . . . . . . . . . . . . . . . . . . . . . . . . . . . . . .

20. . . . . . . . . . . . . . . . . . . . . . . . . . . . . . . . . . . . . . . . . . . . . . . . .

Write down a few sentences on what you would like your closest family member such as partner, parent, sister, brother to say, or would have said, about the life you have lived:-

. . . . . . . . . . . . . . . . . . . . . . . . . . . . . . . . . . . . . . . . . . . . . . . . . .

. . . . . . . . . . . . . . . . . . . . . . . . . . . . . . . . . . . . . . . . . . . . . . . . . .

. . . . . . . . . . . . . . . . . . . . . . . . . . . . . . . . . . . . . . . . . . . . . . . . . .

. . . . . . . . . . . . . . . . . . . . . . . . . . . . . . . . . . . . . . . . . . . . . . . . . .

Write down a few sentences on what you would like your best friend to say or would have said about the life you have lived:-

. . . . . . . . . . . . . . . . . . . . . . . . . . . . . . . . . . . . . . . . . . . . . . . . . .

. . . . . . . . . . . . . . . . . . . . . . . . . . . . . . . . . . . . . . . . . . . . . . . . . .

. . . . . . . . . . . . . . . . . . . . . . . . . . . . . . . . . . . . . . . . . . . . . . . . . .

. . . . . . . . . . . . . . . . . . . . . . . . . . . . . . . . . . . . . . . . . . . . . . . . . .

Write down a few sentences on what you would like your work colleagues or employees to say about the life you have lived:-

. . . . . . . . . . . . . . . . . . . . . . . . . . . . . . . . . . . . . . . . . . . . . . . . . .

. . . . . . . . . . . . . . . . . . . . . . . . . . . . . . . . . . . . . . . . . . . . . . . . . .

. . . . . . . . . . . . . . . . . . . . . . . . . . . . . . . . . . . . . . . . . . . . . . . . . .

. . . . . . . . . . . . . . . . . . . . . . . . . . . . . . . . . . . . . . . . . . . . . . . . . .

. . . . . . . . . . . . . . . . . . . . . . . . . . . . . . . . . . . . . . . . . . . . . . . . . .

What will you say yourself about your life 25 years from now?

. . . . . . . . . . . . . . . . . . . . . . . . . . . . . . . . . . . . . . . . . . . . . . . . . .

. . . . . . . . . . . . . . . . . . . . . . . . . . . . . . . . . . . . . . . . . . . . . . . . . .

. . . . . . . . . . . . . . . . . . . . . . . . . . . . . . . . . . . . . . . . . . . . . . . . . .

. . . . . . . . . . . . . . . . . . . . . . . . . . . . . . . . . . . . . . . . . . . . . . . . . .

# 3 – CLARIFY YOUR CORE LIFE VALUES

To create anything in life, you need to have a strong foundation. As you create the life you love, values are your foundation.

Values are who you are, and not who you would like to be, nor who you think you should be. These are called core values and there are many, of which some are unique to us. Examples are integrity, contribution, service, zest, joy, creativity, independence, beauty, and trust. You will have your own list.

You must dig deep to identify your life values.

**Are you living a life of integrity – that is a life in which your daily words and actions match your beliefs?**

You cannot be true to yourself unless you know who you are. So many of us go through life without taking the time to identify what truly matters to us. It is only when you clarify what really matters to you and what you stand for that you can be free to live life to the full, with more zest, fulfilment, balance – and less stress.

In recent years, I have become clear about my own values – since my life is all about service and contribution, integrity is very important. To me integrity is being, doing and speaking my truth – and of course owning up anytime when I am not fully speaking or living my truth either with myself or others.

I cringe when I look back on my life where I have not acted with integrity, such as when using a company copying machine to make a pirate copy of a correspondence course borrowed from a friend – in fact I was out of integrity on two counts.

Another key value for me is love. What I do for a living would not be possible without coming from a place of love. It really is remarkable how easy my work becomes and how much my life flows when I come from a place of love and integrity.

I also know that when I have been out of tune with my values, I have felt blocked, and life has felt like a struggle. A while ago I was involved in a potentially huge project, but I never quite got excited by it – I now know that my values were not in sync with those of the project founder.

When you are living your life in harmony with your values, you naturally have more energy, fulfilment, balance, and stress-free living. The standards you set for yourself become the expressions of your values in everyday life.

Your values represent your unique and individual essence and your ultimate way of being and relating to others. Your values are what define you – here are some ways of identifying your values and then living by them. For now, simply begin to think about these and after reading the rest of this section you will find space on the next page to write down your thoughts.

Ask yourself what values are important to you and what you are currently focussing on. When thinking of changing jobs, moving home, planning a holiday, get clear on just what values would be the most important considerations.

To get you started, here's a few examples of values. Add your own to this list.

| | | | |
|---|---|---|---|
| Abundance | Adventure | Art | Authenticity |
| Balance | Beauty | Calmness | Charity |
| Community | Compassion | Courage | Creativity |
| Empathy | Equality | Excellence | Excitement |
| Family | Fitness | Friendship | Freedom of choice |
| Fun and laughter | Generosity | Global peace | Harmony |
| Health | Humour | Independence | Inspiring Others |
| Integrity | Intelligence | Joy | Kindness |
| Knowledge | Leadership | Living your dreams | Love for myself |
| Love for others | Music | Nature | Passion |
| Personal growth | Pleasure | Positive attitude | Quality of life |
| Reliability | Sensuality | Spirituality | Taking risks |
| Tidiness | Time freedom | Trust | Wonder and awe |

It is vital that you also know what core values you would simply NOT let go, no matter what. For example, I would never let go of integrity, truthfulness, and honesty.

**Express your core values as much as possible.**

For example, if being creative is a core value for you, then you could look to express your creativity a lot more in your home and in your work. Create your goals for the future based on the awareness of your values. Find an activity where you feel involved with something that matters, rather than something that doesn't.

Think of situations in your life when you felt truly yourself. Reflect on what was going on in detail, where you were, who was present, and who you were being at that time. Get clear on how you were feeling in that situation and what core values you were expressing then.

When I visited Nirvana School in India, it felt like coming home – I was then fully expressing two of my core values, love, and fun. This was the charity school which I visited for a month a few years ago. Working with children there connected me with my core being – I felt I was the biggest child there!

I had gone as a volunteer to this school which supports poor families and gives their children a chance of a better education. During my time at the school, I made a pledge to support it for the rest of my life to the best of my ability.

Ask yourself if you are expressing your personal values at your workplace. It is now clear to me that when I worked for a bank I was frustrated partly because the values of the organisation were not in line with my own core values.

Imagine you had a magic wand, and you could wake up tomorrow doing your dream work. See if you would then be leading a life in line with your values. When performing any action, look at the bigger picture and check if you are being true to yourself. Use your values to clarify any course of action.

Improve your relationships with everyone in your life based on your value awareness. Rather than trying to change someone's values, have mutual respect for them.

**Getting clear about your values will help you to go out and seek the people, situations and things that support those values. It puts you in charge of your life and you will then be on the way to getting a more fulfilling life.**

## Power Actions to Clarify Your Core Life Values

Note down five occasions, when you really felt truly yourself. What values were you expressing? *For example, you may find dancing very enjoyable – you may then be expressing your fun value.*

1. . . . . . . . . . . . . . . . . . . . . . . . . . . . . . . . . . . . . . . . . . . . . . . . . . . . . .
   . . . . . . . . . . . . . . . . . . . . . . . . . . . . . . . . . . . . . . . . . . . . . . . . . . . . .

2. . . . . . . . . . . . . . . . . . . . . . . . . . . . . . . . . . . . . . . . . . . . . . . . . . . . . .
   . . . . . . . . . . . . . . . . . . . . . . . . . . . . . . . . . . . . . . . . . . . . . . . . . . . . .

3. . . . . . . . . . . . . . . . . . . . . . . . . . . . . . . . . . . . . . . . . . . . . . . . . . . . . .
   . . . . . . . . . . . . . . . . . . . . . . . . . . . . . . . . . . . . . . . . . . . . . . . . . . . . .

4. . . . . . . . . . . . . . . . . . . . . . . . . . . . . . . . . . . . . . . . . . . . . . . . . . . . . .
   . . . . . . . . . . . . . . . . . . . . . . . . . . . . . . . . . . . . . . . . . . . . . . . . . . . . .

5. . . . . . . . . . . . . . . . . . . . . . . . . . . . . . . . . . . . . . . . . . . . . . . . . . . . . .
   . . . . . . . . . . . . . . . . . . . . . . . . . . . . . . . . . . . . . . . . . . . . . . . . . . . . .

List 10 core values that you feel represent who you truly are.

1. . . . . . . . . . . . . . . . . . . . . . . . . . . . . . . . . . . . . . . . . . . . . . . . . . . . . .

2. . . . . . . . . . . . . . . . . . . . . . . . . . . . . . . . . . . . . . . . . . . . . . . . . . . . . .

3. . . . . . . . . . . . . . . . . . . . . . . . . . . . . . . . . . . . . . . . . . . . . . . . . . . . . .

4. . . . . . . . . . . . . . . . . . . . . . . . . . . . . . . . . . . . . . . . . . . . . . . . . . . . . .

5. . . . . . . . . . . . . . . . . . . . . . . . . . . . . . . . . . . . . . . . . . . . . . . . . . . . . .

6. . . . . . . . . . . . . . . . . . . . . . . . . . . . . . . . . . . . . . . . . . . . . . . . . . . . . .

7. . . . . . . . . . . . . . . . . . . . . . . . . . . . . . . . . . . . . . . . . . . . . . . . . . . . . .

8. . . . . . . . . . . . . . . . . . . . . . . . . . . . . . . . . . . . . . . . . . . . . . . . . . . . . .

9. . . . . . . . . . . . . . . . . . . . . . . . . . . . . . . . . . . . . . . . . . . . . . . . . . . . . .

10. . . . . . . . . . . . . . . . . . . . . . . . . . . . . . . . . . . . . . . . . . . . . . . . . . . . . .

Describe five things you will do in the next seven days, to bring more of your values into your life. *For example, if fun is a core value for you, look at how you can bring more fun into your life.*

1. . . . . . . . . . . . . . . . . . . . . . . . . . . . . . . . . . . . . . . . . . . . . . . . . .

. . . . . . . . . . . . . . . . . . . . . . . . . . . . . . . . . . . . . . . . . . . . . . . . .

2. . . . . . . . . . . . . . . . . . . . . . . . . . . . . . . . . . . . . . . . . . . . . . . . . .

. . . . . . . . . . . . . . . . . . . . . . . . . . . . . . . . . . . . . . . . . . . . . . . . .

3. . . . . . . . . . . . . . . . . . . . . . . . . . . . . . . . . . . . . . . . . . . . . . . . . .

. . . . . . . . . . . . . . . . . . . . . . . . . . . . . . . . . . . . . . . . . . . . . . . . .

4. . . . . . . . . . . . . . . . . . . . . . . . . . . . . . . . . . . . . . . . . . . . . . . . . .

. . . . . . . . . . . . . . . . . . . . . . . . . . . . . . . . . . . . . . . . . . . . . . . . .

5. . . . . . . . . . . . . . . . . . . . . . . . . . . . . . . . . . . . . . . . . . . . . . . . . .

. . . . . . . . . . . . . . . . . . . . . . . . . . . . . . . . . . . . . . . . . . . . . . . . .

List some areas where you feel that currently you are not living your values. Write down what you will do in the next seven days to change this. *For example, if integrity is a core value for you, own up to those areas in your life where you are not in integrity and decide what you will do to correct this.*

. . . . . . . . . . . . . . . . . . . . . . . . . . . . . . . . . . . . . . . . . . . . . . . . . . .

. . . . . . . . . . . . . . . . . . . . . . . . . . . . . . . . . . . . . . . . . . . . . . . . . . .

. . . . . . . . . . . . . . . . . . . . . . . . . . . . . . . . . . . . . . . . . . . . . . . . . . .

. . . . . . . . . . . . . . . . . . . . . . . . . . . . . . . . . . . . . . . . . . . . . . . . . . .

. . . . . . . . . . . . . . . . . . . . . . . . . . . . . . . . . . . . . . . . . . . . . . . . . . .

. . . . . . . . . . . . . . . . . . . . . . . . . . . . . . . . . . . . . . . . . . . . . . . . . . .

. . . . . . . . . . . . . . . . . . . . . . . . . . . . . . . . . . . . . . . . . . . . . . . . . . .

. . . . . . . . . . . . . . . . . . . . . . . . . . . . . . . . . . . . . . . . . . . . . . . . . . .

. . . . . . . . . . . . . . . . . . . . . . . . . . . . . . . . . . . . . . . . . . . . . . . . . . .

. . . . . . . . . . . . . . . . . . . . . . . . . . . . . . . . . . . . . . . . . . . . . . . . . . .

# 4 - FIND YOUR LIFE PURPOSE

**W**hat's the purpose of your life? Do you live a life in line with your personal values, desires, and dreams?

Your purpose is the essence of what you contribute to the world, simply by virtue of who you are – rather than because of what you know, own, or can do. Knowing your purpose gives you a sense of significance and will propel you to create a life that you love and deserve.

Without a clearly defined purpose and direction, you are easily distracted. Your day gets taken up by lots of irrelevant details and actions and you may find that you constantly work hard but never really get anywhere. Not surprisingly, you become easily discouraged, suffer from a lack of motivation, and start a lot of projects that don't ever get finished.

Once you know your underlying purpose, it focuses you. Everything you do from there onwards stems from that overall purpose. The goals you set will be in harmony with that driving purpose in your life.

Today, more and more people are actively looking for and managing to find their life purpose and there is no reason why you cannot be one of them.

I have met some remarkable individuals such as a landscape painter, a gardener and a doctor who have discovered their purpose. Their lives became magical as everything they did came from their overall purpose.

I discovered my life purpose through spending a lot of time in self-reflection, looking at my life and noting the times when I was happiest, and by talking to some people who knew me well. I knew that serving others was my purpose because it felt so right, and it was so me.

**To truly live your life to the full, you must know what you want to do.**

You must love doing it and you must believe in what you are doing. Your conviction, your enthusiasm, your belief in what you are doing is what will bring you fully alive and this will be noticed by those around you.

Connect with your passion. Reflect on what you are doing on those occasions when you lose all track of time and awareness, whether at home, at work, or anywhere else. What really makes you come live? What contribution do you want to make to the world? What unique talents do you have to offer the world?

Identify your special gifts. These are your unique skills and abilities, which convert your purpose into behaviour and action. They are the abilities you have naturally learned and developed. Remember, there is no other person like you on this planet – you are truly unique.

I feel one of my unique talents is to work with children and – I discovered this passion when a few years ago I spent four weeks at Nirvana School, a charity school in South India. In hindsight, I should have become a school teacher! I now embrace this passion for working with children by coaching children, and by actively supporting children's charities.

As well as being passionate about working with children, one of my gifts is to bring people together for fun social events as well as business events. Someone once asked why I enjoyed doing this so much. Well, for me bringing people together is a God-given gift – but it would not be a 'gift' if I did not share it. Also, I get a lot of joy and satisfaction out of seeing so many people together.

What gifts do you have for the world and which you are not yet sharing? When will you begin? For now, simply begin to think about these and after reading this section you will find space on the next page to write down your thoughts.

Each one of us has a significant contribution to make in our lifetime and this is your higher purpose. The challenge for you is to identify, acknowledge and then express this purpose in your life. Sit quietly and do a creative visualisation exercise to design your dream life.

This is when in your mind's eye using your imagination, you 'see' all those things you would like to be, do, and have. Ask what your dream work would be if you were doing it right now.

Reflect on the things you value. For example, if it is money you value, then ask what it will bring you. Keep going deeper like this and soon you will arrive at your very basic values and your purpose in life. All your desires stem from your deep-down, fundamental values and purpose, and the way to discover them is simply to probe deeper until they are revealed.

Imagine that you are 80 years old, and a big party is being thrown for you. What achievements would you want to be celebrating, as you look back on your life? What would you need to have done, for you to feel that you have fulfilled your life purpose? What legacy do you want to leave behind?

Only a few years ago, we threw a birthday party for an uncle who had reached the age of one hundred. He was probably even older, as a century ago in India no one kept accurate records. At the party there were five generations present and in total my uncle had over 80 direct descendants there. He certainly had a lot to celebrate in his life – his legacy to us was an example of a life of solid graft and helping others. He remains a role model for the four generations that shared his life span.

Look at your childhood dreams and ask what you wanted to do with your life when you grew up. You probably lost touch with your life purpose as you grew older, often due to social conditioning and the gradual loss of your creative self.

Define clearly what success in life means for you. This will indicate what is important to you, and just how you want to lead your life. Ultimately, it will help you identify your way of being.

Look at the bigger picture of your life. Review the decisions and choices you have made, your passion and where you have been and where you are going now. What patterns can you see?

For example, I only realised recently that everything I did – coaching, charity work, writing, public speaking, organising social events – all had a common theme of people and children. Knowing this allows me to continue to come from a place of resonance with my life purpose.

**Knowing and living your purpose helps you make key decisions based on fulfilment and contribution to the world. You live your life with gratitude, passion, and confidence.**

# Power Actions to Find Your Life Purpose

Write down the five things that you are most passionate about.

1. . . . . . . . . . . . . . . . . . . . . . . . . . . . . . . . . . . . . . . . . . . . . .

. . . . . . . . . . . . . . . . . . . . . . . . . . . . . . . . . . . . . . . . . . . . .

2. . . . . . . . . . . . . . . . . . . . . . . . . . . . . . . . . . . . . . . . . . . . . .

. . . . . . . . . . . . . . . . . . . . . . . . . . . . . . . . . . . . . . . . . . . . .

3. . . . . . . . . . . . . . . . . . . . . . . . . . . . . . . . . . . . . . . . . . . . . .

. . . . . . . . . . . . . . . . . . . . . . . . . . . . . . . . . . . . . . . . . . . . .

4. . . . . . . . . . . . . . . . . . . . . . . . . . . . . . . . . . . . . . . . . . . . . .

. . . . . . . . . . . . . . . . . . . . . . . . . . . . . . . . . . . . . . . . . . . . .

5. . . . . . . . . . . . . . . . . . . . . . . . . . . . . . . . . . . . . . . . . . . . . .

. . . . . . . . . . . . . . . . . . . . . . . . . . . . . . . . . . . . . . . . . . . . .

Make a list of 10 of your unique skills and abilities.

1. . . . . . . . . . . . . . . . . . . . . . . . . . . . . . . . . . . . . . . . . . . . . .

2. . . . . . . . . . . . . . . . . . . . . . . . . . . . . . . . . . . . . . . . . . . . . .

3. . . . . . . . . . . . . . . . . . . . . . . . . . . . . . . . . . . . . . . . . . . . . .

4. . . . . . . . . . . . . . . . . . . . . . . . . . . . . . . . . . . . . . . . . . . . . .

5. . . . . . . . . . . . . . . . . . . . . . . . . . . . . . . . . . . . . . . . . . . . . .

6. . . . . . . . . . . . . . . . . . . . . . . . . . . . . . . . . . . . . . . . . . . . . .

7. . . . . . . . . . . . . . . . . . . . . . . . . . . . . . . . . . . . . . . . . . . . . .

8. . . . . . . . . . . . . . . . . . . . . . . . . . . . . . . . . . . . . . . . . . . . . .

9. . . . . . . . . . . . . . . . . . . . . . . . . . . . . . . . . . . . . . . . . . . . . .

10. . . . . . . . . . . . . . . . . . . . . . . . . . . . . . . . . . . . . . . . . . . . . .

If you had a magic wand and you could wake up tomorrow, doing your dream work, what would that be?

. . . . . . . . . . . . . . . . . . . . . . . . . . . . . . . . . . . . . . . . . . . . . . . .

. . . . . . . . . . . . . . . . . . . . . . . . . . . . . . . . . . . . . . . . . . . . . . . .

. . . . . . . . . . . . . . . . . . . . . . . . . . . . . . . . . . . . . . . . . . . . . . . .

. . . . . . . . . . . . . . . . . . . . . . . . . . . . . . . . . . . . . . . . . . . . . . . .

. . . . . . . . . . . . . . . . . . . . . . . . . . . . . . . . . . . . . . . . . . . . . . . .

. . . . . . . . . . . . . . . . . . . . . . . . . . . . . . . . . . . . . . . . . . . . . . . .

It is your 80th birthday party. What three or more key achievements would you want to be celebrating as you look back on your life?

1. . . . . . . . . . . . . . . . . . . . . . . . . . . . . . . . . . . . . . . . . . . . . .

. . . . . . . . . . . . . . . . . . . . . . . . . . . . . . . . . . . . . . . . . . . . .

2. . . . . . . . . . . . . . . . . . . . . . . . . . . . . . . . . . . . . . . . . . . . . .

. . . . . . . . . . . . . . . . . . . . . . . . . . . . . . . . . . . . . . . . . . . . .

3. . . . . . . . . . . . . . . . . . . . . . . . . . . . . . . . . . . . . . . . . . . . . .

. . . . . . . . . . . . . . . . . . . . . . . . . . . . . . . . . . . . . . . . . . . . .

What would you need to have done, for you to feel that you have fully lived your life purpose? What legacy do you want to leave behind?

. . . . . . . . . . . . . . . . . . . . . . . . . . . . . . . . . . . . . . . . . . . . . . . .

. . . . . . . . . . . . . . . . . . . . . . . . . . . . . . . . . . . . . . . . . . . . . . . .

. . . . . . . . . . . . . . . . . . . . . . . . . . . . . . . . . . . . . . . . . . . . . . . .

. . . . . . . . . . . . . . . . . . . . . . . . . . . . . . . . . . . . . . . . . . . . . . . .

. . . . . . . . . . . . . . . . . . . . . . . . . . . . . . . . . . . . . . . . . . . . . . . .

. . . . . . . . . . . . . . . . . . . . . . . . . . . . . . . . . . . . . . . . . . . . . . . .

. . . . . . . . . . . . . . . . . . . . . . . . . . . . . . . . . . . . . . . . . . . . . . . .

# 5 – SET INSPIRING LIFE GOALS

To create the life you love and live it, you must set goals for your life. Do you know what you want to create and have in your life?

Being clear about your goals, writing them down and making them part of your present life, will achieve amazing results. Your goals must be in alignment with your values, your integrity, and your life purpose. I find that once I am clear about my goal and it is in line with who I am, I become almost unstoppable.

A friend once described me as being a bit like a bull terrier – once clear and focussed on achieving something, I become relentless and just don't let go until I have reached my objective. An example of this is when I first created the website for Nirvana school a few years ago. I taught myself the website programme, wrote lots of pages and created the whole website in just a weekend with hardly any sleep. That project became one of the most satisfying things I have ever done, with the website enabling the school to raise a lot of money in donations and sponsorship for the Nirvana children.

Whilst fundraising at the Richoux café, in St Johns Wood, the idea of a book began to emerge. From there it was a mere five weeks, to the moment I had a hard copy in my hands. I worked relentlessly until I had achieved my objective – I just knew that nothing was going to stop me from having my book published.

Write down your goals. There is far more chance of making them happen once they are written down, even if you do not do anything about it consciously. Write them in big bold letters and hang up next to your computer, by your bedside and anywhere else, where you can't fail to see them several times a day. Spend some quality time on your own and reflect on the goals in all areas of your life – short, medium, and long term. Consider where you want to be in three months, one year and three years' time. For now, just reflect on these and at the end of this section you will have an opportunity to write them down.

For me, one of my major goal achievements has been to write this book – this had been a major goal since the age of fifteen. My English teacher at school encouraged me to write more and to even consider following a career in writing – I eventually became a computer specialist instead. That desire to write remained though, and I can now cross off 'writing a book' from my list of life goals. My next writing related goal and one that truly inspires me, is to make this book a bestseller worldwide...

Word your goals creatively, to bring them alive and make them inspirational. Make them SMART. To show you what I mean by this, take my goal of getting the first edition of my book (then called 'Get a Life') published.

| | |
|---|---|
| **Specific** | I wanted to write and publish a book called 'Get a Life'. |
| **Measurable** | I would know I had succeeded when I had a copy of the book in my hands. |
| **Achievable** | I had the ideas, resources, and connections to make it happen. |

| | |
|---|---|
| **Realistic** | I checked with my editor – the time schedule was very tight but was just possible. |
| **Time based** | I wanted it published by the end of November that year, in time for Christmas. |

Making your goals SMART will then help you clearly identify what you want, how badly you want it, whether it is feasible, how you will know when you have got it, and by when you will have achieved it.

Phrase your goals positively. State what you want, not what you don't want. For example, smokers rather than saying they want to quit smoking, could instead say 'I now breath freely once again as a non-smoker'.

Review the goals that you have already achieved in your life and get present to them. Know that you are fully capable of achieving things in your life when you put your mind to it.

At times of any self-doubt, I write in a journal and review all the things I have already achieved in my lifetime, both minor as well as major. This writing exercise helps me become aware once again of my own abilities, skills, and achievements - and it boosts my self-belief. In my journal I now have over 100 achievements. Indeed, it is a good idea to write in a journal all the time and not just when you are in self-doubt. Start your own journal today – you will soon be surprised just how much you have already achieved and created in your life.

Always carry a notebook, with your goals written in it. Wherever you go, write down ideas as they come to you, even whilst you are out and about taking a walk, or in a coffee shop. Of course, you must follow up these ideas with purposeful action. Remember that those people who achieve their goals are not cleverer, or have better contacts, or influence than you – they simply do more towards achieving their goals.

Eliminate any doubts and fears about goal setting. For many people, the goal doesn't happen and that may well be because their internal resistance is so high. Reducing this internal resistance will therefore increase your desire to set goals, as well as boosting your confidence about achieving your goals.

Create a to-do list daily – this is after all your goals list for that day. The to-do list is task based, whilst goals are more specifically related to a vision or dream. Ensure that your daily tasks are in line with your longer-term goals but make sure that you identify the single one most important thing you must do that day and you do this first before starting anything else.

Also, review the to-do list and decide what actions must be done that day – and see if you can drop the rest. Consider creating a 'will-do' list for the day – those things that you will get done, come what may, and this will naturally be a much shorter list. Be realistic with how much you can do each day – do not unduly put pressure on yourself.

Look at your goals in terms of the benefits they will give you once achieved. Write down these benefits against each goal. If ever you falter, this list of benefits will help to keep you motivated. Remember to think about the actions you need to do to get your goals moving.

Keep the end goal in mind. Do not give up because the goal doesn't happen. Start to believe that you will achieve your goals and that goal setting does work.

**Goals without any action are just dreams – but goals that you act upon become dreams with deadlines.**

## Power Actions to Set Inspiring Life Goals

Write down five goals you have already achieved in your life that you are proud of.

1. . . . . . . . . . . . . . . . . . . . . . . . . . . . . . . . . . . . . . . . . . . . . . . . . .

   . . . . . . . . . . . . . . . . . . . . . . . . . . . . . . . . . . . . . . . . . . . . . . . . .

2. . . . . . . . . . . . . . . . . . . . . . . . . . . . . . . . . . . . . . . . . . . . . . . . . .

   . . . . . . . . . . . . . . . . . . . . . . . . . . . . . . . . . . . . . . . . . . . . . . . . .

3. . . . . . . . . . . . . . . . . . . . . . . . . . . . . . . . . . . . . . . . . . . . . . . . . .

   . . . . . . . . . . . . . . . . . . . . . . . . . . . . . . . . . . . . . . . . . . . . . . . . .

4. . . . . . . . . . . . . . . . . . . . . . . . . . . . . . . . . . . . . . . . . . . . . . . . . .

   . . . . . . . . . . . . . . . . . . . . . . . . . . . . . . . . . . . . . . . . . . . . . . . . .

5. . . . . . . . . . . . . . . . . . . . . . . . . . . . . . . . . . . . . . . . . . . . . . . . . .

   . . . . . . . . . . . . . . . . . . . . . . . . . . . . . . . . . . . . . . . . . . . . . . . . .

Write down in detail the one goal that you must achieve in your lifetime.

. . . . . . . . . . . . . . . . . . . . . . . . . . . . . . . . . . . . . . . . . . . . . . . . . . .

. . . . . . . . . . . . . . . . . . . . . . . . . . . . . . . . . . . . . . . . . . . . . . . . . . .

. . . . . . . . . . . . . . . . . . . . . . . . . . . . . . . . . . . . . . . . . . . . . . . . . . .

. . . . . . . . . . . . . . . . . . . . . . . . . . . . . . . . . . . . . . . . . . . . . . . . . . .

. . . . . . . . . . . . . . . . . . . . . . . . . . . . . . . . . . . . . . . . . . . . . . . . . . .

. . . . . . . . . . . . . . . . . . . . . . . . . . . . . . . . . . . . . . . . . . . . . . . . . . .

. . . . . . . . . . . . . . . . . . . . . . . . . . . . . . . . . . . . . . . . . . . . . . . . . . .

. . . . . . . . . . . . . . . . . . . . . . . . . . . . . . . . . . . . . . . . . . . . . . . . . . .

. . . . . . . . . . . . . . . . . . . . . . . . . . . . . . . . . . . . . . . . . . . . . . . . . . .

. . . . . . . . . . . . . . . . . . . . . . . . . . . . . . . . . . . . . . . . . . . . . . . . . . .

. . . . . . . . . . . . . . . . . . . . . . . . . . . . . . . . . . . . . . . . . . . . . . . . . . .

. . . . . . . . . . . . . . . . . . . . . . . . . . . . . . . . . . . . . . . . . . . . . . . . . . .

. . . . . . . . . . . . . . . . . . . . . . . . . . . . . . . . . . . . . . . . . . . . . . . . . . .

. . . . . . . . . . . . . . . . . . . . . . . . . . . . . . . . . . . . . . . . . . . . . . . . . . .

Write down three short term goals you want to have achieved in three months' time.

1. . . . . . . . . . . . . . . . . . . . . . . . . . . . . . . . . . . . . . . . . . . . . . . . . . . .
2. . . . . . . . . . . . . . . . . . . . . . . . . . . . . . . . . . . . . . . . . . . . . . . . . . . .
3. . . . . . . . . . . . . . . . . . . . . . . . . . . . . . . . . . . . . . . . . . . . . . . . . . . .

What three specific actions will you take in the next seven days, towards these short term goals?

1. . . . . . . . . . . . . . . . . . . . . . . . . . . . . . . . . . . . . . . . . . . . . . . . . . . .
2. . . . . . . . . . . . . . . . . . . . . . . . . . . . . . . . . . . . . . . . . . . . . . . . . . . .
3. . . . . . . . . . . . . . . . . . . . . . . . . . . . . . . . . . . . . . . . . . . . . . . . . . . .

Write down three medium term goals you want to achieve in a year's time.

1. . . . . . . . . . . . . . . . . . . . . . . . . . . . . . . . . . . . . . . . . . . . . . . . . . . .
2. . . . . . . . . . . . . . . . . . . . . . . . . . . . . . . . . . . . . . . . . . . . . . . . . . . .
3. . . . . . . . . . . . . . . . . . . . . . . . . . . . . . . . . . . . . . . . . . . . . . . . . . . .

What three specific actions will you take in the next fourteen days, towards your medium term goals?

1. . . . . . . . . . . . . . . . . . . . . . . . . . . . . . . . . . . . . . . . . . . . . . . . . . . .
2. . . . . . . . . . . . . . . . . . . . . . . . . . . . . . . . . . . . . . . . . . . . . . . . . . . .
3. . . . . . . . . . . . . . . . . . . . . . . . . . . . . . . . . . . . . . . . . . . . . . . . . . . .

Write down three long term goals you want to achieve in three years' time.

1. . . . . . . . . . . . . . . . . . . . . . . . . . . . . . . . . . . . . . . . . . . . . . . . . . . .
2. . . . . . . . . . . . . . . . . . . . . . . . . . . . . . . . . . . . . . . . . . . . . . . . . . . .
3. . . . . . . . . . . . . . . . . . . . . . . . . . . . . . . . . . . . . . . . . . . . . . . . . . . .

What three specific actions will you take in the next month, towards your long term goals?

1. . . . . . . . . . . . . . . . . . . . . . . . . . . . . . . . . . . . . . . . . . . . . . . . . . . .
2. . . . . . . . . . . . . . . . . . . . . . . . . . . . . . . . . . . . . . . . . . . . . . . . . . . .
3. . . . . . . . . . . . . . . . . . . . . . . . . . . . . . . . . . . . . . . . . . . . . . . . . . . .

# 6 - CLEAR ALL THE CLUTTER FROM YOUR LIFE

**B**efore you can start to get the life you love, you need to have a clear space in which to create something significant.

To move forward in your life, you must simplify and clear out all those things from the past that are holding you back. I have found that clutter clearing is the single one thing that makes the biggest difference to my coaching clients and enables them to move towards a life they love.

**The simpler and more streamlined your life is, the more space and time you will have to fully focus on what you want to create in your life.**

I had one coaching client who with her husband had so many old souvenirs and presents accumulated from a lifetime together that they had to hire a storage warehouse in the countryside, just to store everything. They enthusiastically took on the idea of clearing up their lives and within just a few weeks, they were able to empty the warehouse, and benefit from no longer having to pay a hefty rent for the warehouse. She also cleared up the clutter from their house and in her own words she felt like a 'new person'.

I was once helping my late father with some paperwork, and I was amused and shocked to find 25 years' worth of old TV licences! My father had kept them in case anyone ever knocked on the door demanding to see his licence. Reluctantly he did agree to throw them out, but it was quite a challenge to get him to dump decades' worth of old cheque book stubs!

Clutter is not just those physical things hoarded for years. It includes relationships, social media, time commitments and other things that use up more of your energy than you can afford to give them.

Is your home full of things you no longer use? Do you have so many commitments that you don't have quality time for anything? Are you surrounded by people who drain you? If so, then perhaps it is time you reviewed what they add to your life and what they are taking away.

Ask yourself why you are holding on to something. Old school reports or a gift you were given years ago and have never used are taking up valuable space so be honest about why you have still got them. Ask yourself if it is sentimental, or just laziness, you will have your own reasons. Get clear on what it is that you are resisting giving up and what you are afraid of letting go. Just imagine all the goodness that is simply waiting to come into your life when you make space for it.

The great benefit of cleaning up your life is that it boosts your energy levels since you are no longer wasting time and mental thoughts on things not of importance to you. You can then focus on the things that really matter.

A few years ago, after I became single again, I had a blitz of all my worldly belongings and cleared out the usual things such as ornaments, photographs, books, clothes, files on my computer and paperwork. I even created a new set of friends who supported and nurtured me in my new life, and I let go of a lot of old friendships. Everything I removed from my life around that time enabled me to begin creating a new life that was much more in alignment with who I am now.

Today in my home everything is either functional, beautiful or has some sentimental value – or all three. Anything that no longer fits these criteria soon goes out of my home and out of my life. Conversely, anything new that now comes into my home must fit my criteria. Also, since every item has a place or a home where it belongs, it also makes my life so easy and simple. And as I periodically review my home space once a month, my life stays that way.

**Get started on doing the same with your life today - go through your entire house, one room or area at a time.**

Enrol the help of a friend if you feel that would help. Decide what to throw out, give away, store, sell or keep. A good rule of thumb is to get rid of everything you absolutely do not need or have not used in the last 12 months.

Start your clutter clearing with just one small area, in one room at a time. Go through your kitchen cupboards and discard all those old tins that have been there for years. Empty the fridge of out-of-date half-used items.

Clear up those things that rob you of your time. Watch less television. Go outdoors more often and enjoy the fresh air.

Review your friends. Ask yourself: What am I getting out of this friendship? Does this person lift my energy? Do I love being in his or her company? Begin to gently let go today of any friendships that no longer support and nurture you. In the past I have done this by gradually being less and less in touch with people who I felt no longer supported me in my new life or who seemed to drain me. It was a natural process of drifting apart and one day they were no longer in my life.

Be gentle and considerate as you clear up your life. Keep only the things that support you in your chosen lifestyle, and which give you joy and reflect your values. Do not let the clutter build up again. Assign a place to everything that you wish to keep. Watch your time commitments to other people and ensure that you only spend as little or as much time as you want with others. Do not make any promises without giving due thought and consideration of what will be required from you.

Have some fun whilst clearing things from your home and do reward yourself afterwards. For example, listen to your favourite music whilst you work, or have some friends around and have a clutter clearing party. In return you can do the same for them. Perhaps you can schedule a meal afterwards to celebrate your achievement and to say thank you for the help you have received.

**Clearing out the physical clutter will create a space for new things to come into your life.**

Another area that you must declutter and simplify is your social media – review and minimise the time you spend on your electronic gadgets.

Do you have a lot of Facebook "friends" who drain you? Are you wasting hours and hours on mindless surfing on Instagram and TikTok, and getting sucked into toxic debates on Twitter?

Draw up some strict guidelines for yourself on how much time you will spend daily on your digital devices. Develop the discipline to not have your phone by your bedside at night-time.

The best thing you can do with your mobile phone and other devices is to leave them in a different room whilst working or spending quality time with your loved ones. Model this behaviour for children and other people in your life. Remember, people want and crave your presence.

It's quite a challenge to review and minimise the time you spend on social media and on your devices, but you can do it. See it as a game and challenge yourself to win every day.

**Simplifying your life is one of the most powerful things you can do for your peace of mind, and for your growth.**

# Power Actions to Clear All the Clutter from Your Life

To help you identify areas for clearing your clutter answer YES or NO to these questions.

1. Do you hang on to clothes that no longer fit you?
2. Do you have in your wardrobe items bought years ago and not worn since?
3. Do you own shoes that hurt your feet?
4. Do you own spectacles for old prescriptions?
5. Do you have toiletries or cosmetics which have dried up or are half finished?
6. Do you have a pile of papers /unopened mail/junk mail/emails awaiting action or filing?
7. Do you have a pin-board with more than one layer of papers on it?
8. Do you keep old newspapers or magazines as there is an article you want to read?
9. Do you have so many books there is not enough room on your shelves?
10. Do you own kitchen gadgets or digital devices you never use?
11. Do you have a drawer stuffed full of plastic shopping bags?
12. Do you have half-finished projects stashed around the house?
13. Do you have hundreds of photos in boxes, unfiled or not put together in some order?
14. Do you have old medicines and pills stored in a cupboard?
15. Do you have things awaiting repairs for months?
16. Do you keep things purely because they were a gift?
17. Do you keep things in case one day they come in handy?
18. Do things fall out of your cupboards when you open the doors?
19. Do you have problems finding things just when you want them?
20. Do you have in your kitchen any items in cupboards or fridge/freezer past their use by dates?
21. Do you have old digital files, images, and programs on your computer?
22. Do you have out-of-date contacts, old images and unused apps on your phone and other digital devices?
23. Do you have a backlog of emails, digital files, web links and social media notifications to go through?
24. Do you get overwhelmed with all the social media messages, notifications, and digital news bombarding you daily?

Wherever you have said YES is an area for clutter clearing. Start clearing out this area TODAY, even if you get rid of just one item.

List 10 things that you can clear out of your house and office in the next seven days. Gather them all up and take to a charity shop or recycling centre. Alternatively, give the items to someone who you know needs them. Also find a good home for unwanted office items. Do it this week.

1. . . . . . . . . . . . . . . . . . . . .        6. . . . . . . . . . . . . . . . . . . . . . . . .

2. . . . . . . . . . . . . . . . . . . . .        7. . . . . . . . . . . . . . . . . . . . . . . . .

3. . . . . . . . . . . . . . . . . . . . .        8. . . . . . . . . . . . . . . . . . . . . . . . .

4. . . . . . . . . . . . . . . . . . . . .        9. . . . . . . . . . . . . . . . . . . . . . . . .

5. . . . . . . . . . . . . . . . . . . . .        10. . . . . . . . . . . . . . . . . . . . . . . .

Go through your commitments to other people over the next two weeks and review them. What three commitments can you drop?

1. . . . . . . . . . . . . . . . . . . . . . . . . . . . . . . . . . . . . . . . . . . . . . . . . . . . .

2. . . . . . . . . . . . . . . . . . . . . . . . . . . . . . . . . . . . . . . . . . . . . . . . . . . . .

3. . . . . . . . . . . . . . . . . . . . . . . . . . . . . . . . . . . . . . . . . . . . . . . . . . . . .

Go through each of these areas in your home. Write a date against each area, by which time you will have cleared the clutter.

Living room. . . . . . . . . . . . .        Hallway . . . . . . . . . . . . . . . . . . . . . . . .

Study / Office . . . . . . . . . . . .        Bathroom . . . . . . . . . . . . . . . . . . . . . . . .

Bedroom 1 . . . . . . . . . . . . . .        Bedroom 2 . . . . . . . . . . . . . . . . . . . . . .

Bedroom 3 . . . . . . . . . . . . . .        Bedroom 4 . . . . . . . . . . . . . . . . . . . . . .

Kitchen . . . . . . . . . . . . . . . .        Garage . . . . . . . . . . . . . . . . . . . . . . . . .

Shed . . . . . . . . . . . . . . . . . .        Garden. . . . . . . . . . . . . . . . . . . . . . . . .

Car . . . . . . . . . . . . . . . . . . . .

Other areas . . . . . . . . . . . . . .

. . . . . . . . . . . . . . . . . . . . . . .

. . . . . . . . . . . . . . . . . . . . . . .

# 7 - BUILD UP YOUR SELF-ESTEEM

**W**hen creating the life you love, do you believe that you deserve the best? Do you believe in yourself, or do you suffer from low self-esteem?

In my work, I meet some very capable people with a lot going for them and yet they have such low self-esteem. Quite often major life changing events bring this about.

When my marriage collapsed a few years ago, for a while I went out partying heavily and got into a crowd of people not necessarily good for me. I also stopped taking self-care and became very sloppy in my outlook and my appearance. I now know that this was due to low self-esteem and a desire to be with people who accepted me. I was looking for validation outside of me.

In recent years, I have done a lot of self-development work on myself and probably now have more self-esteem than ever before in my life. This in turn has enabled me to follow my life purpose and pursue my goals.

**Positive self-esteem will empower you to meet life's challenges, and to consider yourself worthy of happiness.**

Focusing on your positive traits will immediately improve your chances of creating the life you desire and deserve. Stop putting yourself down from now on as you cannot develop high self-esteem when you repeat negative thoughts and phrases about yourself and your abilities.

Look at your past successes and achievements. Make a list of 20 things you have done. These don't have to be major achievements. They can include things like learning to ride a bike, passing your driving test, getting promoted at work, learning a new skill, passing an exam, or doing something new that challenges you.

I had always been a very happy child full of positive self-esteem. I brimmed with confidence and was considered very bright academically. At the age of twelve, I was graded as one of the top 10 students out of almost 8,000 pupils nationwide who sat the Kenyan equivalent of the eleven-plus examination.

Somewhere along the way, I lost my self-belief and subsequently in my academic career, I only performed 'average' by my own high perceived standards. I was actually very hard on myself and began to consider myself as 'mediocre'. But what kept me going and got me to where I am today was the awareness and appreciation of all my successes and my positive qualities.

Next time you feel low, just remember the times when you were proud of what you did, and the times you were praised. Close your eyes and recreate those feelings of satisfaction and joy that you experienced.

Stop comparing yourself with other people as there will always be people who have achieved more than you, and some who have less. Instead, observe positive confident people around you. By looking at what they do and how they behave, you can copy them as role models for how you would like to be. For example, if they are confident, and you feel you are not, see how they walk into a room, or speak to people, and do the same. If you are habitually saying negative things and they are very positive, turn that round in yourself.

Think of at least 10 of your positive qualities of which you are proud. For instance, you may be reliable, honest, helpful, imaginative or any number of other characteristics. Write these on a piece of brightly coloured paper and stick it up where you will see it regularly – perhaps on your mirror, office wall or the fridge door. Read this list, at least once every day.

Ask five people, who know you well, to write down your top five perceived strengths. Prepare to be pleasantly surprised as I was when I began my training as a coach. The first seven friends to whom I mentioned my new career all said they felt that coaching was so in tune with me and that I was born to do just that. They saw me as having everything I needed to serve others with transforming their lives.

**Always remember that you have infinite value to offer to the world.**

Review your negative beliefs and ask if these beliefs are true. Actively look for evidence to disprove your negative beliefs. For instance, if you believe you can't speak confidently in public ask yourself these questions:

**Is this belief helpful to you?**

**Where did this limiting belief come from?**

**What would you rather believe instead?**

Once you have those answers you can create a new empowering belief. Write down what the benefits would be of the new positive belief. For example, I used to think that I was shy and could not speak well in public. This came about partly as my school classmates teased me relentlessly about my African accent when I arrived in the UK from Kenya. I replaced this limiting belief with a belief that what I have to say is important and people will want to listen to me.

Begin to accept yourself as you are. Look in the mirror every morning and say: "I love and approve of myself". This may seem awkward but keep repeating until you can look yourself in the eye and mean it.

Do something good for somebody else. It could be as simple as helping an elderly person to cross the road or giving up your seat on public transport for someone who looks tired or is pregnant. Doing things for others will automatically create self-esteem. For example, working with Nirvana school, the children's school in South India, does make me feel very good about myself, though that is not the main purpose for being involved in the school.

Associate with people who energise you and appreciate your positive points. When you are surrounded by negative people who constantly put you down, your self-esteem is lowered. Conversely, when you are accepted and encouraged, you feel better about yourself.

**As you begin to create the life you love, remember that you deserve the best that life has to offer.**

# Power Actions to Build Up Your Self-Esteem

Write down up to 20 things you have achieved in your lifetime so far.

1. . . . . . . . . . . . . . . . . . . . . . . . . . . . . . . . . . . . . . . . . . . . . . . . . . . . . .
2. . . . . . . . . . . . . . . . . . . . . . . . . . . . . . . . . . . . . . . . . . . . . . . . . . . . . .
3. . . . . . . . . . . . . . . . . . . . . . . . . . . . . . . . . . . . . . . . . . . . . . . . . . . . . .
4. . . . . . . . . . . . . . . . . . . . . . . . . . . . . . . . . . . . . . . . . . . . . . . . . . . . . .
5. . . . . . . . . . . . . . . . . . . . . . . . . . . . . . . . . . . . . . . . . . . . . . . . . . . . . .
6. . . . . . . . . . . . . . . . . . . . . . . . . . . . . . . . . . . . . . . . . . . . . . . . . . . . . .
7. . . . . . . . . . . . . . . . . . . . . . . . . . . . . . . . . . . . . . . . . . . . . . . . . . . . . .
8. . . . . . . . . . . . . . . . . . . . . . . . . . . . . . . . . . . . . . . . . . . . . . . . . . . . . .
9. . . . . . . . . . . . . . . . . . . . . . . . . . . . . . . . . . . . . . . . . . . . . . . . . . . . . .
10. . . . . . . . . . . . . . . . . . . . . . . . . . . . . . . . . . . . . . . . . . . . . . . . . . . . . .
11. . . . . . . . . . . . . . . . . . . . . . . . . . . . . . . . . . . . . . . . . . . . . . . . . . . . . .
12. . . . . . . . . . . . . . . . . . . . . . . . . . . . . . . . . . . . . . . . . . . . . . . . . . . . . .
13. . . . . . . . . . . . . . . . . . . . . . . . . . . . . . . . . . . . . . . . . . . . . . . . . . . . . .
14. . . . . . . . . . . . . . . . . . . . . . . . . . . . . . . . . . . . . . . . . . . . . . . . . . . . . .
15. . . . . . . . . . . . . . . . . . . . . . . . . . . . . . . . . . . . . . . . . . . . . . . . . . . . . .
16. . . . . . . . . . . . . . . . . . . . . . . . . . . . . . . . . . . . . . . . . . . . . . . . . . . . . .
17. . . . . . . . . . . . . . . . . . . . . . . . . . . . . . . . . . . . . . . . . . . . . . . . . . . . . .
18. . . . . . . . . . . . . . . . . . . . . . . . . . . . . . . . . . . . . . . . . . . . . . . . . . . . . .
19. . . . . . . . . . . . . . . . . . . . . . . . . . . . . . . . . . . . . . . . . . . . . . . . . . . . . .
20. . . . . . . . . . . . . . . . . . . . . . . . . . . . . . . . . . . . . . . . . . . . . . . . . . . . . .

List up to five of your major successes.  What does this tell you about yourself?

1. ................................................................

    ................................................................

2. ................................................................

    ................................................................

3. ................................................................

    ................................................................

4. ................................................................

    ................................................................

5. ................................................................

    ................................................................

Write down up to 10 things you really like about yourself.

1. ................................................................

2. ................................................................

3. ................................................................

4. ................................................................

5. ................................................................

6. ................................................................

7. ................................................................

8. ................................................................

9. ................................................................

10. ................................................................

# 8 – APPRECIATE ALL THE ABUNDANCE AROUND YOU

**A**s you create the life you love, you have so much abundance around you to help you do so.

Abundance is a lot more than just money or material things. You live in a very rich and beautiful world – just open your eyes. Think about the beauty of the sky, the greenery all around you, the grace of animals, the love within you, the miracle of life.

As I write this in the summer, I am sitting in a park in central London, the sun is shining, there are birds singing in the background and I am surrounded by lush trees and rose bushes.

**Do you live in a world of abundance? Or do you come from a place of scarcity and lack?**

It is your choice, whether to see the world through the eyes of abundance or lack. It is a choice that you make, based on your conditioning and beliefs. Change your perception, and even more abundance will flow into your life in many forms, from love and money to worldly goods.

Begin to appreciate just how much abundance there is all around you. Count your blessings and be thankful for the goodness already in your life. Just for today, show gratitude to every living thing. And then do the same every day from now on.

I have owned large properties and fast cars and though I have moved away from them, I consider myself to have even more abundance than ever before in terms of the life I now lead, the people in my life and the work I do. At the time, those material things mattered, and they still do, but I now know there is much more to my abundance.

Be generous, without being wasteful. Always remember that what goes around comes around. In other words, what you give out, you get back so share the abundance already in your life and it will be reflected back to you by others. Freely share your home, worldly goods, time, and love, without expectations of anything in return.

I recently gifted a friend the use of my home and garden for a weekend healing workshop. I expected nothing in return but was pleased when one of the attendees at the workshop kindly referred some promising business leads. I now expect gifts to come to me in unexpected ways and it felt wonderful that through my initial generosity, I was given in return something of higher value, and of long-term benefit to me.

A few years ago, when I cut down on drinking alcohol, it felt great to be able to gift some liquor bottles to the porters in my apartment building. Those drinks would have otherwise simply stagnated in my kitchen.

There is a story of a couple who saved a bottle of champagne from their wedding day to celebrate on a special occasion. Twelve years later they opened it only to find it had turned into vinegar!

From now onwards, look for opportunities of savouring and sharing your abundance today, rather than waiting for one day, some day in the future.

Plant seeds of abundance all around you. Consider allotting a certain percentage, say 10 per cent, of your income to charitable causes. Do this anonymously, and without any expectation of recognition.

Simplify your life in all ways. Begin to enjoy the simple things in life, such as walks in nature, playtime with children, and sharing special meals with your loved ones.

**Become aware, every second, of just how much joy there is in your life.**

Let go of any habits of poverty. Start giving away your loose change to charities and people in need. Start cultivating being prosperous. Stop thinking thoughts such as I can't afford that.

Always be kind and loving towards yourself. Pamper yourself with lots of little treats such as your favourite drink in a special glass, a relaxing bath with oils and candles, or a meal at your favourite restaurant. Do whatever does it for you.

Expect the best from everything and everyone. Pessimistic people who are always moaning keep having negative experiences and bad luck. That is because what you focus on most is what you create – so focus only on goodness from now on. Think of the things you love and desire.

Take time to be still. Meditation, yoga and walks in the park will all help to keep you grounded and calm. Find what works for you and stick to it. Never beat yourself up for slipping into any old habits of negativity or lack of appreciation. Simply forgive yourself and move on.

**You can develop powerful and life-enhancing habits over time – just be patient with yourself and see how your life transforms rapidly.**

Recall a time in your life when you felt a deep sense of richness and completeness. Remember how you felt and get present to these feelings once again. Know that you can recreate those feelings of abundance anytime you wish to do so.

From today onwards, consciously think, feel, and identify with happy thoughts of abundance. Begin each day by being thankful for everything you can think of.

**As you get and live the life you love, always remember what an abundant world we live in.**

# Power Actions to Appreciate All the Abundance Around You

Note down up to 20 examples of abundance in your life.

1. . . . . . . . . . . . . . . . . . . . . . . . . . . . . . . . . . . . . . . . . . . . . .

2. . . . . . . . . . . . . . . . . . . . . . . . . . . . . . . . . . . . . . . . . . . . . .

3. . . . . . . . . . . . . . . . . . . . . . . . . . . . . . . . . . . . . . . . . . . . . .

4. . . . . . . . . . . . . . . . . . . . . . . . . . . . . . . . . . . . . . . . . . . . . .

5. . . . . . . . . . . . . . . . . . . . . . . . . . . . . . . . . . . . . . . . . . . . . .

6. . . . . . . . . . . . . . . . . . . . . . . . . . . . . . . . . . . . . . . . . . . . . .

7. . . . . . . . . . . . . . . . . . . . . . . . . . . . . . . . . . . . . . . . . . . . . .

8. . . . . . . . . . . . . . . . . . . . . . . . . . . . . . . . . . . . . . . . . . . . . .

9. . . . . . . . . . . . . . . . . . . . . . . . . . . . . . . . . . . . . . . . . . . . . .

10. . . . . . . . . . . . . . . . . . . . . . . . . . . . . . . . . . . . . . . . . . . . . .

11. . . . . . . . . . . . . . . . . . . . . . . . . . . . . . . . . . . . . . . . . . . . . .

12. . . . . . . . . . . . . . . . . . . . . . . . . . . . . . . . . . . . . . . . . . . . . .

13. . . . . . . . . . . . . . . . . . . . . . . . . . . . . . . . . . . . . . . . . . . . . .

14. . . . . . . . . . . . . . . . . . . . . . . . . . . . . . . . . . . . . . . . . . . . . .

15. . . . . . . . . . . . . . . . . . . . . . . . . . . . . . . . . . . . . . . . . . . . . .

16. . . . . . . . . . . . . . . . . . . . . . . . . . . . . . . . . . . . . . . . . . . . . .

17. . . . . . . . . . . . . . . . . . . . . . . . . . . . . . . . . . . . . . . . . . . . . .

18. . . . . . . . . . . . . . . . . . . . . . . . . . . . . . . . . . . . . . . . . . . . . .

19. . . . . . . . . . . . . . . . . . . . . . . . . . . . . . . . . . . . . . . . . . . . . .

20. . . . . . . . . . . . . . . . . . . . . . . . . . . . . . . . . . . . . . . . . . . . . .

List up to 10 things that give you much joy.

1. . . . . . . . . . . . . . . . . . . . . . . . . . . . . . . . . . . . . . . . . . . . . . . . . . . .

2. . . . . . . . . . . . . . . . . . . . . . . . . . . . . . . . . . . . . . . . . . . . . . . . . . . .

3. . . . . . . . . . . . . . . . . . . . . . . . . . . . . . . . . . . . . . . . . . . . . . . . . . . .

4. . . . . . . . . . . . . . . . . . . . . . . . . . . . . . . . . . . . . . . . . . . . . . . . . . . .

5. . . . . . . . . . . . . . . . . . . . . . . . . . . . . . . . . . . . . . . . . . . . . . . . . . . .

6. . . . . . . . . . . . . . . . . . . . . . . . . . . . . . . . . . . . . . . . . . . . . . . . . . . .

7. . . . . . . . . . . . . . . . . . . . . . . . . . . . . . . . . . . . . . . . . . . . . . . . . . . .

8. . . . . . . . . . . . . . . . . . . . . . . . . . . . . . . . . . . . . . . . . . . . . . . . . . . .

9. . . . . . . . . . . . . . . . . . . . . . . . . . . . . . . . . . . . . . . . . . . . . . . . . . . .

10. . . . . . . . . . . . . . . . . . . . . . . . . . . . . . . . . . . . . . . . . . . . . . . . . . .

Describe five things you will do in the next seven days, to enjoy and share your abundance with others. *For example, giving loose change to charity, sharing your personal things, sending a surprise gift, buying a stranger a drink.*

1. . . . . . . . . . . . . . . . . . . . . . . . . . . . . . . . . . . . . . . . . . . . . . . . . . . .

. . . . . . . . . . . . . . . . . . . . . . . . . . . . . . . . . . . . . . . . . . . . . . . . . . .

2. . . . . . . . . . . . . . . . . . . . . . . . . . . . . . . . . . . . . . . . . . . . . . . . . . . .

. . . . . . . . . . . . . . . . . . . . . . . . . . . . . . . . . . . . . . . . . . . . . . . . . . .

3. . . . . . . . . . . . . . . . . . . . . . . . . . . . . . . . . . . . . . . . . . . . . . . . . . . .

. . . . . . . . . . . . . . . . . . . . . . . . . . . . . . . . . . . . . . . . . . . . . . . . . . .

4. . . . . . . . . . . . . . . . . . . . . . . . . . . . . . . . . . . . . . . . . . . . . . . . . . . .

. . . . . . . . . . . . . . . . . . . . . . . . . . . . . . . . . . . . . . . . . . . . . . . . . . .

5. . . . . . . . . . . . . . . . . . . . . . . . . . . . . . . . . . . . . . . . . . . . . . . . . . . .

. . . . . . . . . . . . . . . . . . . . . . . . . . . . . . . . . . . . . . . . . . . . . . . . . . .

## 9 – GIVE AND RECEIVE OPENLY

As you create a life you love, you will be helped and supported by many different people. You cannot easily do it on your own. There will be a lot of giving and taking, supporting each other and teamwork.

Do you look to serve others in any way you can? Or do you tend to look out just for yourself?

I was once asked by a friend why I wanted to help her so much – at the time I simply replied that I didn't know. Today I would say to her that I needed no reason to serve her or indeed serve anyone. I hope she is reading this today and can now understand where I was coming from.

I also learnt the distinction between fixing, helping, and serving. People don't need fixing as they are perfectly whole and complete as they are – and they are fully capable of helping themselves. Once you can accept this, you can adopt a service mindset and look to ways of serving all those around you.

This was a big insight for me in my early coaching career as I was trying to help and forcefully "fix" everyone. That's changed for me now as I come from a place of service.

You have a choice in how you behave towards others. You can be generous, considerate, and caring to the people around you - or you can be selfish, self-centred, and always put your own interests first.

Gifts come to us in all shapes and sizes every minute of the day, if only we can become open to acknowledging and receiving them. Every human interaction is an opportunity for giving and receiving a gift for our learning and growth. The gift may be love, friendship, honesty, support, thoughtfulness, generosity, humour, fun. What goes around comes around, and you will receive as surely as you give.

**Trust that all is well, and that things are evolving in perfect harmony.**

For me this happened beautifully when I ran a 'coaching café' at my local coffee shop in St John's Wood, called Richoux, to help Comic Relief. The local press covered my efforts and even carried a photograph of me wearing a red wig and a red nose! This in turn led to a regular coaching column in their weekly paper. And the words from my weekly articles eventually became the foundation for this book. From today onwards, look to contribute in any way you can, and be prepared for it all to come back to you in all kinds of ways.

The learning for me in my life has been to see the gift in every situation, especially when the 'gift' has been a surprise or not even wanted! I went through the most painful time in my life when my ex-wife and I parted, and our marriage ended. I now know and appreciate that it was a wonderful gift to each other when we decided to part ways so we could both be true to ourselves and be the people we were meant to be.

For many people, giving is the easy part whilst it is in receiving that we can close down or refuse the gift. You must be open to receiving because if everyone was giving, and no one was receiving, to whom would you be giving?

Recognise that by being open to receiving, you are giving the other person an opportunity to be blessed by their giving. It is a great thing to both give and to receive. Though people saw me as very generous and a great giver, I used to have great difficulty in receiving gifts. I have now become much more open in recent years, and I simply keep telling myself that I deserve to receive from others.

When you give to another, you receive the blessings of what you have given them – such as pleasure, satisfaction, and joy. This way of giving and receiving is all about balance, and once you put it into action, you will receive as surely as you give. See every interaction as a gift – where you can learn and grow, and whereby you help others to grow too. Mentally imagine giving a gift every time you meet someone. Ask yourself – what can I do for this person?

A sincere compliment or even just acknowledging a person's presence can make a huge difference to them – and you. Do not confuse giving compliments with flattery. Compliments should be positive, sincere, and focused on something specific. For example, 'You look radiant today'.

Get like-minded people together and connect those whom you feel may have some potential to benefit each other. Recommend someone's services or products. Help other people grow through your recommendations. Offer to put people in touch with someone who you think could help them. Recommend the plumber or decorator who did such a great job for you.

Say something positive to at least three people every day. This could be your neighbour, a work colleague, or a shop assistant. The opportunities of brightening up someone's day are endless once you begin to look out for them. Smile and see how others respond. Give someone the gift of your smile and kindness. It is amazing how easily you can lift someone's spirits with a smile.

Offer help to someone lost or in trouble. Look for any person in distress. Even giving directions to a lost tourist will lift your own spirits – not to mention theirs.

Serve someone for no other reason than to make their life easier. For example, next time you are stuck in a traffic queue, smile, and give way to other motorists. Make a monetary contribution to a good cause. A little change can go a long way.

**Get into the habit of saying only positive things about other people.**

To help you become aware of all your giving and receiving, keep a 'Give and Get' book. Get a thick notebook and in the pages at the front write down daily all the things you are giving. In the pages at the back, write down all the things you are getting. You will be amazed how quickly the pages fill up and you may find that giving, receiving, and acknowledging your gifts can be fun and fulfilling.

Get present to all the gifts in your life, small or big; surprising or unwanted. By unwanted, I mean unexpected turn of events, criticism, anger, as well as unsuitable objects. Receive the gift, acknowledge it and be grateful. Remember to also express your heartfelt thanks for any unwanted 'gifts'.

Remember, in every relationship you are a gift bearer and a gift receiver. And a key to creating the life you love is a service mindset and contribution.

**Begin contributing and giving openly today. Make adopting a service mindset a lifelong mission – your life will change dramatically and your interactions with other people will become more fulfilling, enjoyable, and fun.**

## Power Actions to Give and Receive Openly

Imagine that **contribution** is your lifelong mission from now on. What would you be doing? Whom can you serve right now?

. . . . . . . . . . . . . . . . . . . . . . . . . . . . . . . . . . . . . . . . . . . . . . . . . . . .

. . . . . . . . . . . . . . . . . . . . . . . . . . . . . . . . . . . . . . . . . . . . . . . . . . . .

. . . . . . . . . . . . . . . . . . . . . . . . . . . . . . . . . . . . . . . . . . . . . . . . . . . .

. . . . . . . . . . . . . . . . . . . . . . . . . . . . . . . . . . . . . . . . . . . . . . . . . . . .

. . . . . . . . . . . . . . . . . . . . . . . . . . . . . . . . . . . . . . . . . . . . . . . . . . . .

. . . . . . . . . . . . . . . . . . . . . . . . . . . . . . . . . . . . . . . . . . . . . . . . . . . .

. . . . . . . . . . . . . . . . . . . . . . . . . . . . . . . . . . . . . . . . . . . . . . . . . . . .

. . . . . . . . . . . . . . . . . . . . . . . . . . . . . . . . . . . . . . . . . . . . . . . . . . . .

. . . . . . . . . . . . . . . . . . . . . . . . . . . . . . . . . . . . . . . . . . . . . . . . . . . .

. . . . . . . . . . . . . . . . . . . . . . . . . . . . . . . . . . . . . . . . . . . . . . . . . . . .

List 10 things you can do for other people in the next 14 days. *For example, give way to other motorists when waiting in traffic, donate clothes or money to a charity, send some flowers to a neighbour.*

1. . . . . . . . . . . . . . . . . . . . . . . . . . . . . . . . . . . . . . . . . . . . . . . . .

2. . . . . . . . . . . . . . . . . . . . . . . . . . . . . . . . . . . . . . . . . . . . . . . . .

3. . . . . . . . . . . . . . . . . . . . . . . . . . . . . . . . . . . . . . . . . . . . . . . . .

4. . . . . . . . . . . . . . . . . . . . . . . . . . . . . . . . . . . . . . . . . . . . . . . . .

5. . . . . . . . . . . . . . . . . . . . . . . . . . . . . . . . . . . . . . . . . . . . . . . . .

6. . . . . . . . . . . . . . . . . . . . . . . . . . . . . . . . . . . . . . . . . . . . . . . . .

7. . . . . . . . . . . . . . . . . . . . . . . . . . . . . . . . . . . . . . . . . . . . . . . . .

8. . . . . . . . . . . . . . . . . . . . . . . . . . . . . . . . . . . . . . . . . . . . . . . . .

9. . . . . . . . . . . . . . . . . . . . . . . . . . . . . . . . . . . . . . . . . . . . . . . . .

10. . . . . . . . . . . . . . . . . . . . . . . . . . . . . . . . . . . . . . . . . . . . . . . . .

List five people whose services you can recommend to other people in the next seven days. *For example, John the builder who installed your kitchen.*

1. . . . . . . . . . . . . . . . . . . . . . . . . . . . . . . . . . . . . . . . . . . . . . . . . . . .
   . . . . . . . . . . . . . . . . . . . . . . . . . . . . . . . . . . . . . . . . . . . . . . . . . . .

2. . . . . . . . . . . . . . . . . . . . . . . . . . . . . . . . . . . . . . . . . . . . . . . . . . . .
   . . . . . . . . . . . . . . . . . . . . . . . . . . . . . . . . . . . . . . . . . . . . . . . . . . .

3. . . . . . . . . . . . . . . . . . . . . . . . . . . . . . . . . . . . . . . . . . . . . . . . . . . .
   . . . . . . . . . . . . . . . . . . . . . . . . . . . . . . . . . . . . . . . . . . . . . . . . . . .

4. . . . . . . . . . . . . . . . . . . . . . . . . . . . . . . . . . . . . . . . . . . . . . . . . . . .
   . . . . . . . . . . . . . . . . . . . . . . . . . . . . . . . . . . . . . . . . . . . . . . . . . . .

5. . . . . . . . . . . . . . . . . . . . . . . . . . . . . . . . . . . . . . . . . . . . . . . . . . . .
   . . . . . . . . . . . . . . . . . . . . . . . . . . . . . . . . . . . . . . . . . . . . . . . . . . .

List three positive things about five people in your life. *For example, Miriam who is always helping others with her skill, making meals for those in need and willing to act as a taxi when needed.*

1. . . . . . . . . . . . . . . . . . . . . . . . . . . . . . . . . . . . . . . . . . . . . . . . . . . .
   . . . . . . . . . . . . . . . . . . . . . . . . . . . . . . . . . . . . . . . . . . . . . . . . . . .

2. . . . . . . . . . . . . . . . . . . . . . . . . . . . . . . . . . . . . . . . . . . . . . . . . . . .
   . . . . . . . . . . . . . . . . . . . . . . . . . . . . . . . . . . . . . . . . . . . . . . . . . . .

3. . . . . . . . . . . . . . . . . . . . . . . . . . . . . . . . . . . . . . . . . . . . . . . . . . . .
   . . . . . . . . . . . . . . . . . . . . . . . . . . . . . . . . . . . . . . . . . . . . . . . . . . .

4. . . . . . . . . . . . . . . . . . . . . . . . . . . . . . . . . . . . . . . . . . . . . . . . . . . .
   . . . . . . . . . . . . . . . . . . . . . . . . . . . . . . . . . . . . . . . . . . . . . . . . . . .

5. . . . . . . . . . . . . . . . . . . . . . . . . . . . . . . . . . . . . . . . . . . . . . . . . . . .
   . . . . . . . . . . . . . . . . . . . . . . . . . . . . . . . . . . . . . . . . . . . . . . . . . . .

# 10 – BE POSITIVE AND JOYOUS EVERYDAY

**A**s you create the life you love, remaining positive will help you get over any difficulties and delays which might occur.

Have you ever met someone who is always positive, and a joy to be around – someone with lots of energy, and who can see the sunny side to everything? You can be such a person too.

I remember being so infectiously positive in my younger days that it used to drive my friends mad. My energy and enthusiasm spilled over into everything I did, and they had a hard time keeping up with me! I am no less positive nowadays, but I now seem to have added some wisdom learnt over the passing years and my energy is more balanced which makes it easier for others to be around me.

Often you cannot do anything about circumstances, such as the loss of a job or the end of a relationship. It can knock us off balance, but it is how you react that really determines how long you stay down.

**It is not about being naively positive in the midst of dire circumstances, but to be upbeat whilst accepting the situation and being realistic about your options for the way forward.**

I went through the most painful period of my life a few years ago when everything in my life seemed to go wrong at once. The day my wife and I separated was sheer anguish of the sort I never want to go through again. I had also just been made redundant and the flat I lived in only had a few weeks left on its rental agreement. My relationship, job and home were falling away from me.

That day amidst the grief and pain, I made the decision to remain positive and look on the bright side which was quite difficult to say the least. I was helped and supported by some close friends and my family through the challenging months that followed. And only a few years later I led a life that I could hardly have imagined then.

Without denying the trauma and pain of life changing events, it is up to you to decide how you will handle them and get on with your life. It is an old cliché, but when the going gets tough, the tough get going.

**You always have a choice. And you can choose to see the positive side to everything.**

Ask yourself what's the worst thing that could happen, or has happened? Often things that apparently go wrong are a blessing in disguise.

Of course, it is a completely different matter when a loved one has passed away.

When both my mother and my middle brother passed away in 2022 within 5 months of each other, it was a very challenging time for me and my siblings. Somehow I got through that time, and though the deep pain of loss is still there, I am now in acceptance of my loss and in gratitude for all that my mother and brother did for me in my life. I feel their presence all around me.

Many people get a 'wake-up call' through some tragedy – and suddenly their life takes on a new meaning as they grow in previously unimaginable ways. Looking back, I had my wake-up call when I separated from my wife and my marriage folded. This episode in my life made me realise that I had to take responsibility for my own life, and I was the only one who could make me happy. I promised myself that I would never again rely for my happiness on another person or on material belongings.

I also vowed to become a better person all around and not to hurt another human being.

**My key insight was that life is short and I had to make the most of myself for the rest of my life.**

When you feel you have been insulted, or passed over, be willing and ready to forgive. An 'insult' can be as simple as not being acknowledged by a friend or being passed over for promotion.

Know that everyone is doing the best they can, armed only with the awareness, understanding and knowledge that they have at the time. Assume the best of other people.

Forgiveness can take time and effort – but it will bring you relief and healing. Think of who you are willing and able to forgive – and do so. It can be as easy as deciding to forgive them, or it may prove more difficult for you depending on the circumstances. The important thing is you make a start on forgiving and keep on forgiving them.

You may also want to ask for professional help or talk it over with a close friend or family member if the issues you are dealing with are deep seated and painful for you.

When something doesn't go the way you would have liked, ask yourself: Does it really matter? In the great scheme of things, it doesn't really matter if someone cuts you up in the rush hour traffic. Have no expectations about how things should be, and you will lighten up.

**Life is an adventure. Decide that no matter how today turns out, you are going to enjoy whatever the day brings. Each new day brings you an abundance of gifts – open your eyes to them.**

Build up your self-esteem – review all the good things that you have got going in your life and all your achievements to date. Include 'minor' achievements too such as learning to use the computer for sending emails, being able to cook simple dishes and playing basic tunes on the piano.

Stop dwelling on the past and begin to work on your present circumstances. The present will ultimately help you create the future that you seek. Learn key lessons from the past and then move on.

Learn to chill out and have fun. Laughter, playfulness, and relaxation are beneficial to the mind as well as the body. By having some fun in your life, you will have a positive effect on such things as how rapidly you age, your immune system and how your body reacts to stress. You will also learn to see potentially stressful situations as challenges or opportunities and not as insoluble problems.

To create and live the life you love, stay focused on your goals, and keep the motivation going. Adopt a 'can do' attitude. Cultivate a belief in your ability to cope with whatever life may bring.

**Above all, be enthusiastic about life and all that it brings – and remember – life is an adventure.**

## Power Actions to Become Positive and Joyous Everyday

List five 'negative' things that have happened to you, which in hindsight have turned out to be blessings in disguise. *Once you have done this, resolve to see all events from now on as positive experiences.*

1. . . . . . . . . . . . . . . . . . . . . . . . . . . . . . . . . . . . . . . . . . . . . .
   . . . . . . . . . . . . . . . . . . . . . . . . . . . . . . . . . . . . . . . . . . . . .

2. . . . . . . . . . . . . . . . . . . . . . . . . . . . . . . . . . . . . . . . . . . . . .
   . . . . . . . . . . . . . . . . . . . . . . . . . . . . . . . . . . . . . . . . . . . . .

3. . . . . . . . . . . . . . . . . . . . . . . . . . . . . . . . . . . . . . . . . . . . . .
   . . . . . . . . . . . . . . . . . . . . . . . . . . . . . . . . . . . . . . . . . . . . .

4. . . . . . . . . . . . . . . . . . . . . . . . . . . . . . . . . . . . . . . . . . . . . .
   . . . . . . . . . . . . . . . . . . . . . . . . . . . . . . . . . . . . . . . . . . . . .

5. . . . . . . . . . . . . . . . . . . . . . . . . . . . . . . . . . . . . . . . . . . . . .
   . . . . . . . . . . . . . . . . . . . . . . . . . . . . . . . . . . . . . . . . . . . . .

Think of up to five people in your life whom you can forgive. What will you do to forgive them? *For example, have a conversation with them, write them a letter.*

1. . . . . . . . . . . . . . . . . . . . . . . . . . . . . . . . . . . . . . . . . . . . . .
   . . . . . . . . . . . . . . . . . . . . . . . . . . . . . . . . . . . . . . . . . . . . .

2. . . . . . . . . . . . . . . . . . . . . . . . . . . . . . . . . . . . . . . . . . . . . .
   . . . . . . . . . . . . . . . . . . . . . . . . . . . . . . . . . . . . . . . . . . . . .

3. . . . . . . . . . . . . . . . . . . . . . . . . . . . . . . . . . . . . . . . . . . . . .
   . . . . . . . . . . . . . . . . . . . . . . . . . . . . . . . . . . . . . . . . . . . . .

4. . . . . . . . . . . . . . . . . . . . . . . . . . . . . . . . . . . . . . . . . . . . . .
   . . . . . . . . . . . . . . . . . . . . . . . . . . . . . . . . . . . . . . . . . . . . .

5. . . . . . . . . . . . . . . . . . . . . . . . . . . . . . . . . . . . . . . . . . . . . .
   . . . . . . . . . . . . . . . . . . . . . . . . . . . . . . . . . . . . . . . . . . . . .

What five negative things in your life can you give up right now? *For example: I could stop saying 'no I can't do that'.*

1. . . . . . . . . . . . . . . . . . . . . . . . . . . . . . . . . . . . . . . . . . . . . . . . . . . .

   . . . . . . . . . . . . . . . . . . . . . . . . . . . . . . . . . . . . . . . . . . . . . . . . . . .

2. . . . . . . . . . . . . . . . . . . . . . . . . . . . . . . . . . . . . . . . . . . . . . . . . . . .

   . . . . . . . . . . . . . . . . . . . . . . . . . . . . . . . . . . . . . . . . . . . . . . . . . . .

3. . . . . . . . . . . . . . . . . . . . . . . . . . . . . . . . . . . . . . . . . . . . . . . . . . . .

   . . . . . . . . . . . . . . . . . . . . . . . . . . . . . . . . . . . . . . . . . . . . . . . . . . .

4. . . . . . . . . . . . . . . . . . . . . . . . . . . . . . . . . . . . . . . . . . . . . . . . . . . .

   . . . . . . . . . . . . . . . . . . . . . . . . . . . . . . . . . . . . . . . . . . . . . . . . . . .

5. . . . . . . . . . . . . . . . . . . . . . . . . . . . . . . . . . . . . . . . . . . . . . . . . . . .

   . . . . . . . . . . . . . . . . . . . . . . . . . . . . . . . . . . . . . . . . . . . . . . . . . . .

What five positive things can you do from now on when you encounter a 'negative' experience? *For example: say 'I may not know how to do that, but I am willing to learn'*

1. . . . . . . . . . . . . . . . . . . . . . . . . . . . . . . . . . . . . . . . . . . . . . . . . . . .

   . . . . . . . . . . . . . . . . . . . . . . . . . . . . . . . . . . . . . . . . . . . . . . . . . . .

2. . . . . . . . . . . . . . . . . . . . . . . . . . . . . . . . . . . . . . . . . . . . . . . . . . . .

   . . . . . . . . . . . . . . . . . . . . . . . . . . . . . . . . . . . . . . . . . . . . . . . . . . .

3. . . . . . . . . . . . . . . . . . . . . . . . . . . . . . . . . . . . . . . . . . . . . . . . . . . .

   . . . . . . . . . . . . . . . . . . . . . . . . . . . . . . . . . . . . . . . . . . . . . . . . . . .

4. . . . . . . . . . . . . . . . . . . . . . . . . . . . . . . . . . . . . . . . . . . . . . . . . . . .

   . . . . . . . . . . . . . . . . . . . . . . . . . . . . . . . . . . . . . . . . . . . . . . . . . . .

5. . . . . . . . . . . . . . . . . . . . . . . . . . . . . . . . . . . . . . . . . . . . . . . . . . . .

   . . . . . . . . . . . . . . . . . . . . . . . . . . . . . . . . . . . . . . . . . . . . . . . . . . .

## 11 – BECOME SELF-CONFIDENT AND FEARLESS

**P**ersonal confidence is the key for so many things. When you are confident, life is easier when meeting new people, giving a presentation, or facing an awkward situation.

Your lack of self-confidence limits you from taking advantage of the opportunities that come your way, and from achieving a lot more. Success in life depends heavily in believing in your own ability to succeed and having a strong sense of self-worth that means you know that you count.

In my younger days, I remember being very confident and feeling that I could do anything. Everything was possible and the world was my oyster.

Years later I became brash and cocky, and others began to perceive me as arrogant. When I realised that was the impression I was giving to others I decided to downplay myself to such a point that I became too self-effacing. I am now quietly confident and secure within myself – and of course the world is still my oyster.

You can develop your self-confidence by being open to learning and growing, and by paying special attention to yourself and those around you. The only thing that is stopping you from becoming the person you want to be is you.

Babies first learn to walk by attempting to take a step or two, falling over and trying again and again, no matter how many times they fall over. And then one day they are walking a few steps at a time.

**Confidence is an outcome, and not a prerequisite before you start on anything new.**

If confidence was needed up front, no baby would ever learn to walk!

A lot of the time you may compare yourselves unfavourably with others. You put yourself down by thinking that you will never be as good as them. Ask yourself what you can learn from the person you are comparing yourself to. What is it they do that you could model, and create their perceived level of success?

Recall the times in your life when you felt highly confident – reconnect with that feeling and know that you can access it again anytime you wish. Get to know yourself. Become aware of your values, strengths, and skills - and how others view you. Get feedback from good friends on how they see you. Listen to them and work on those areas that could be improved.

Develop the confident image that you want to project. Select role models and learn from what they do. I had always wanted to be able to speak well in public, but I held myself back due to lack of confidence in getting started. However, once I got talking, it was usually hard to stop me!

I found some wonderful public speaking mentors to help me with my speaking career -and as modelled and learnt from what they do well, speaking in public became easier.

I also now know that what was holding me back from getting started was bad memories of being bullied and teased relentlessly about my African accent by my classmates when I arrived in England from Kenya as a young boy. Looking back, I was an easy victim for them as I was quite a puny child and being seen by the teachers as the brightest in the class did not help either.

In a funny sort of way, this worked in my favour when I was still at school in Africa. There were only two African boys in my class, and I was very open and sincere towards them, unlike the rest of the pupils. They became my best friends and protected me from the school bullies. Having them as allies instilled more confidence in me.

Improve your image and appearance. Make the most of yourself: get a flattering haircut, manicure your nails, and maintain a healthy skin care regime. Take time with your clothes and shoes. Dress to be professional yet comfortable.

**Focus on the things in your life that are working well, and on your strong points, rather than what you think is not working.**

What are you good at? What can you do that very few others can?

Concentrate on the positive aspects of your life and move away from problems and fears. Continue to clarify where you want to go in your life. Having clarity about your goals and your future will instil confidence in you, and people will sense your assuredness.

Let go of the inner voice that criticises you every time something doesn't quite go your way. Instead, analyse the situation and learn from it. This will help you learn, grow, and move on. Look creatively at setbacks.

Take care of your health and invest quality time in looking after yourself. Eat healthily and exercise regularly. Reward and treat yourself regularly. If you feel good inwardly, you will look good outwardly.

Watch your body language. Present an open, upright, and friendly stance. And smile! People will begin to relate to you more and will feel at ease around you. In turn, you will feel more confident around people.

Stretch yourself, step outside your comfort zone and boost your confidence even further.

**Confidence does not come overnight – build it up step by step and have fun on the way as you create and live the life you love.**

## Power Actions to Become Self-Confident and Fearless

Think of up to five experiences when your confidence level has been high. Remember how you felt then, and feel like that again, right now. Bring that feeling back into your life. Now write down the experiences and feelings so you can refer to them in the future.

1. . . . . . . . . . . . . . . . . . . . . . . . . . . . . . . . . . . . . . . . . . . . . . . . . . . . .
. . . . . . . . . . . . . . . . . . . . . . . . . . . . . . . . . . . . . . . . . . . . . . . . . . . .
. . . . . . . . . . . . . . . . . . . . . . . . . . . . . . . . . . . . . . . . . . . . . . . . . . . .
. . . . . . . . . . . . . . . . . . . . . . . . . . . . . . . . . . . . . . . . . . . . . . . . . . . .

2. . . . . . . . . . . . . . . . . . . . . . . . . . . . . . . . . . . . . . . . . . . . . . . . . . . . .
. . . . . . . . . . . . . . . . . . . . . . . . . . . . . . . . . . . . . . . . . . . . . . . . . . . .
. . . . . . . . . . . . . . . . . . . . . . . . . . . . . . . . . . . . . . . . . . . . . . . . . . . .
. . . . . . . . . . . . . . . . . . . . . . . . . . . . . . . . . . . . . . . . . . . . . . . . . . . .

3. . . . . . . . . . . . . . . . . . . . . . . . . . . . . . . . . . . . . . . . . . . . . . . . . . . . .
. . . . . . . . . . . . . . . . . . . . . . . . . . . . . . . . . . . . . . . . . . . . . . . . . . . .
. . . . . . . . . . . . . . . . . . . . . . . . . . . . . . . . . . . . . . . . . . . . . . . . . . . .
. . . . . . . . . . . . . . . . . . . . . . . . . . . . . . . . . . . . . . . . . . . . . . . . . . . .

4. . . . . . . . . . . . . . . . . . . . . . . . . . . . . . . . . . . . . . . . . . . . . . . . . . . . .
. . . . . . . . . . . . . . . . . . . . . . . . . . . . . . . . . . . . . . . . . . . . . . . . . . . .
. . . . . . . . . . . . . . . . . . . . . . . . . . . . . . . . . . . . . . . . . . . . . . . . . . . .
. . . . . . . . . . . . . . . . . . . . . . . . . . . . . . . . . . . . . . . . . . . . . . . . . . . .

5. . . . . . . . . . . . . . . . . . . . . . . . . . . . . . . . . . . . . . . . . . . . . . . . . . . . .
. . . . . . . . . . . . . . . . . . . . . . . . . . . . . . . . . . . . . . . . . . . . . . . . . . . .
. . . . . . . . . . . . . . . . . . . . . . . . . . . . . . . . . . . . . . . . . . . . . . . . . . . .
. . . . . . . . . . . . . . . . . . . . . . . . . . . . . . . . . . . . . . . . . . . . . . . . . . . .

Talk to three friends and get their feedback on how they see you. Write down the most important points here.

1. ................................................................

   ................................................................

2. ................................................................

   ................................................................

3. ................................................................

   ................................................................

List three role models that you admire. What special qualities do they have, that you can emulate?

1. ................................................................

   ................................................................

2. ................................................................

   ................................................................

3. ................................................................

   ................................................................

List three things that you will do in the next seven days, to improve your image and appearance.

1. ................................................................

   ................................................................

2. ................................................................

   ................................................................

3. ................................................................

   ................................................................

## 12 - KEEP YOUR COOL AND BECOME PEACEFUL

To create the life you love, you must be able to keep a cool head come what may – especially when the people around you are losing theirs!

I cringe now as I remember how in the past I used to lose my cool and end up driving like a crazy maniac. I am lucky I never ever hit someone or another car especially as at the time I used to drive a sports car. I became a different person, full of rage and for no reason. I had little peace of mind, and such moments of madness were probably my way of letting it all out.

I now know that peace of mind is something you can have all the time. It comes from a combination of many things and once achieved, it sustains you when things are not going well.

**Who you are BEING at any moment is everything – you can be calm, peaceful, and grounded – or you can be anxious, agitated and all over the place.**

Over time, you can develop a way of being which is cool, calm, and collected. Others will also pick up on your peaceful being and will themselves become more peaceful and calmer.

A few years ago, I was attending an important work meeting where things were getting heated and one of my colleagues afterwards commented on how calm and collected I had been and at the same time in control of the meeting. It was at that moment I realised that I had come a long way in my self-control – I was finally able to keep my cool and be at peace with myself.

Sit quietly and breathe naturally. This can be done anywhere, anytime, with your eyes open or closed. Taking long, slow deep breaths signals to your body that you want peace. You might want to practise this whilst driving, with your eyes open of course, or when about to go into an important meeting or before any situation in your life that would normally cause you stress. Check out and experience different types of meditation or yoga. There are so many apps nowadays to help you do just that.

Create quiet time in your life. Schedule one or two blocks of time for 'peace' every week. Allow yourself to just BE and feel the presence of peace all around you. For example, Sunday morning is a sacred time for me, reserved for some peaceful time and self-pampering.

I now start my day with a quiet period of thirty minutes when I might sit listening to some soothing music in my lounge on my comfortable sofa which is covered with a soft, red Indian throw. Some mornings I go for a walk in my local park or sit in my garden under a huge tree, an ancient copper beech tree whose leaves change colour dramatically as the summer progresses. That precious time in the morning sets me up for the day.

Stop trying so hard to fix things – situations, people, and so on. Take a step back and give yourself permission to leave the world as it is. Let go of the things you cannot control. There is nothing to fix!

Quite often, the outcome of a situation is out of your control, no matter how well you execute a plan. Be content to do the very best you can, and then step back.

Do not lose any sleep over small issues – and then learn to view all issues as small issues. Ask yourself: Does this really matter? In the scheme of things, will you even remember this issue in years to come?

Clear your to-do list. Having undone things, deadlines, overdue payments etc. causes stress every time you think about them. Fix a schedule to get rid of them and enlist a friend, a work colleague, a family member, or a coach to keep you on schedule. Just knowing that you are making progress will enhance your peace of mind.

Forgive others and believe in their innate goodness. Remember that most people don't harm others on purpose, and everyone is doing the best they can, with their current level of awareness, knowledge and understanding.

**Accept that you can only ever change yourself and make decisions about your own actions, not those of others. And the only person about whom you have the right to make decisions is yourself.**

Prioritise your commitments and your time. If any activity makes your life a struggle, unload as much of it as you can, or if possible give it up altogether. Eliminate any activity that does not add real value to your life and keep only what matters.

Make your surroundings relaxing and enjoyable. Keep them tidy, organised, and attractive. Involve all your senses – experience music or silence; the smell of incense; the feel of freshly laundered sheets.

People who visit my home comment on how it feels like a peace haven and a retreat. I have achieved this by being very selective and having only those things that are beautiful, nurturing and have a calming effect on me. Look to create a haven in your own home – do whatever works for you.

Get in touch with nature. Have a short walk at least once a day, and if you can, look for a large healthy tree and sit with your back right up against it so you can feel the power of the tree and the earth. If you are near to water then sit by a fountain, ocean, or lake to experience the same feeling. I am lucky to have in my garden a huge ancient copper beech tree and just being around it seems to give everyone a lift.

Take a drive or jump on a train into the country and see lots of trees and maybe even some cows, sheep, or horses. Bask in all that nature – city dwellers especially will find time spent in the country very peaceful and revitalising.

Turn off the lights and use candlelight for a short time. This will immediately put you in a calm mood as candles are a signal for you to slow down and relax. Make the act of lighting candles a ritual for creating and experiencing calmness.

Set yourself up for a peaceful night's sleep and don't relive scenarios from your day – just let the day go. Breathe deeply and as you doze off, think of nothing.

**Keep your cool and be at peace – it will help you appreciate and fully live your life even more.**

## Power Actions to Keep your Cool and Become Peaceful

Stop what you are doing and sit still for 10 minutes, right now. Make it a habit to have two such 10 -minute breaks every day. Gradually increase from 10 minutes to 20 minutes.

Now write down how you felt.

. . . . . . . . . . . . . . . . . . . . . . . . . . . . . . . . . . . . . . . . . . . . . . . . . . . . . .
. . . . . . . . . . . . . . . . . . . . . . . . . . . . . . . . . . . . . . . . . . . . . . . . . . . . . .
. . . . . . . . . . . . . . . . . . . . . . . . . . . . . . . . . . . . . . . . . . . . . . . . . . . . . .
. . . . . . . . . . . . . . . . . . . . . . . . . . . . . . . . . . . . . . . . . . . . . . . . . . . . . .
. . . . . . . . . . . . . . . . . . . . . . . . . . . . . . . . . . . . . . . . . . . . . . . . . . . . . .
. . . . . . . . . . . . . . . . . . . . . . . . . . . . . . . . . . . . . . . . . . . . . . . . . . . . . .
. . . . . . . . . . . . . . . . . . . . . . . . . . . . . . . . . . . . . . . . . . . . . . . . . . . . . .
. . . . . . . . . . . . . . . . . . . . . . . . . . . . . . . . . . . . . . . . . . . . . . . . . . . . . .
. . . . . . . . . . . . . . . . . . . . . . . . . . . . . . . . . . . . . . . . . . . . . . . . . . . . . .
. . . . . . . . . . . . . . . . . . . . . . . . . . . . . . . . . . . . . . . . . . . . . . . . . . . . . .
. . . . . . . . . . . . . . . . . . . . . . . . . . . . . . . . . . . . . . . . . . . . . . . . . . . . . .

Reflect on some of the issues in your life, which currently bother you. Ask yourself if they really matter. Are you trying to fix something? Is the outcome yours to control? Make them all small issues and let them go.

. . . . . . . . . . . . . . . . . . . . . . . . . . . . . . . . . . . . . . . . . . . . . . . . . . . . . .
. . . . . . . . . . . . . . . . . . . . . . . . . . . . . . . . . . . . . . . . . . . . . . . . . . . . . .
. . . . . . . . . . . . . . . . . . . . . . . . . . . . . . . . . . . . . . . . . . . . . . . . . . . . . .
. . . . . . . . . . . . . . . . . . . . . . . . . . . . . . . . . . . . . . . . . . . . . . . . . . . . . .
. . . . . . . . . . . . . . . . . . . . . . . . . . . . . . . . . . . . . . . . . . . . . . . . . . . . . .
. . . . . . . . . . . . . . . . . . . . . . . . . . . . . . . . . . . . . . . . . . . . . . . . . . . . . .
. . . . . . . . . . . . . . . . . . . . . . . . . . . . . . . . . . . . . . . . . . . . . . . . . . . . . .
. . . . . . . . . . . . . . . . . . . . . . . . . . . . . . . . . . . . . . . . . . . . . . . . . . . . . .
. . . . . . . . . . . . . . . . . . . . . . . . . . . . . . . . . . . . . . . . . . . . . . . . . . . . . .
. . . . . . . . . . . . . . . . . . . . . . . . . . . . . . . . . . . . . . . . . . . . . . . . . . . . . .

Write down up to five things that you will start doing in the next fourteen days that will bring you more peace in your life. *Consider walks in nature, meditation, yoga, clearing up any work backlog, organising your space, clutter clearing and forgiving someone.*

1. ........................................................

   ........................................................

2. ........................................................

   ........................................................

3. ........................................................

   ........................................................

4. ........................................................

   ........................................................

5. ........................................................

   ........................................................

Write down up to five things that you will STOP doing in the next fourteen days that will bring you more peace in your life.

1. ........................................................

   ........................................................

2. ........................................................

   ........................................................

3. ........................................................

   ........................................................

4. ........................................................

   ........................................................

5. ........................................................

   ........................................................

## 13 – STRIVE FOR EXCELLENCE ALWAYS

**A**s you create the life you love, you can strive for excellence, rather than doing just enough to get by.

Accomplishing tasks in an exemplary fashion gives you great pride and self-esteem, since how you do things is a measure of how you rate yourself. Always use your talents, abilities, and skills in the best way possible. Get ahead by giving that little bit extra and by simply doing your best in everything you do at work, home, and play.

The Japanese are renowned for their 'Kaizen' principle – continuous and on-going improvement at everything they do – see how you can bring this approach into all areas of your life.

I used to play a lot of squash at one time, and I became determined to be as good as I possibly could be at this game. I ended up playing competitively up to four times a week. The game became an obsession, and I even hired a squash coach.

I became extremely fit and reached a very high standard. I now bring the same level of drive and commitment to excel in other areas of my life, such as in my coaching work.

Always give more than is expected of you, regardless of what's in it for you. Exceed expectations and go the extra mile. Look at every situation in terms of adding value. Do things faster, better, and even more cheerfully for everyone in your life – customers, employer, family, and for yourself. Over the years I seem to have obtained a reputation for doing things well for everyone in my life – and I have consciously worked at doing things to the best of my ability. I invite you to do the same.

Have a passion for whatever you do for a living because if you don't, then you will only be putting in minimum effort and your half-hearted attempts will ultimately show up as mediocrity. Seek out those things you can get passionate about and use them to create excellence in your life.

**Believe that what you do matters, and that it will make a difference. A life of fulfilment comes from seeking to contribute as much as you can.**

You can't save the whole world single-handedly, and we can't all be a Gandhi or a Mandela, but you can certainly make a difference to one person at a time.

Always look for ways to contribute. Ask yourself what special skill or knowledge you have that can solve a problem or make the best of a situation so that it would serve and support others.

Remember also that striving for excellence does not mean you must be perfect. Sometimes, instead of trying something new that I wasn't sure I would be any good at, I wouldn't even attempt starting it. I have had to learn to let go of this drive to be the best at everything I do, without of course compromising on my standards.

When I was playing squash regularly, I did get very frustrated as after a while I noticed my game had stopped improving. That is when my squash coach was able to point out a few simple changes in my technique that took my game up another level.

What simple changes do you need to make in the way you do things?

Challenge yourself to excel all the time. Aim high and push to be your absolute best – then go even beyond that. You are capable of far more than you think. At the same time, be realistic – do not set your sights so high that you have no way of reaching your goal. Do not set yourself up for failure.

Be totally committed to what you do, as excellence is only possible with commitment. Either get fully committed to what you're doing or find something else to do and commit to.

Expect the best from yourself. Talk to yourself only in positive terms and eliminate all negative self-talk. Similarly, expect the best of everyone around you and generally you will get the best from them. For example, when at a restaurant, being polite and respectful towards the waiters and expecting good service usually means that you get just that. Similarly, you get the best service from shop assistants when you expect the best of them.

Always follow through and follow up. Just a little more effort to finish off a job will bring big results. Conversely, start only what you know you can finish. Doing it right first time around will also save you a lot of time in not having to go back and fix it later.

**Focus on one thing at a time and plan your time so that you can give each task your undivided attention. You will be amazed how much you can get done.**

Block out any distractions such as television, mobile phone, social media, email, visitors, and so on. Ask yourself – what's more important – the goal or the distraction?

Take extreme care of yourself as being at your best, physically and mentally, will give you the energy, drive, and vitality to excel. Take regular breaks. Work diligently while you are at it – and then put it aside. Have regular vacations and reflect on bringing even more excellence into your life.

Learn from every experience – every situation has a learning opportunity – see problems and obstacles as opportunities to grow and excel. Learn what you can from it. Learn from others and appreciate excellence whenever you come across it.

See any criticism as a gift of feedback. Of course, if you have a highly critical partner or boss, or you work with a particularly unhelpful colleague, then you may have to ponder deeper for the learning in the situation.

Use all available tools and resources such as computers, the internet, books, and helpful software like accountancy packages. Get clear on what you want to excel at, and you are then more likely to find someone or something that will help you. Focus on getting any help you can so that you can excel.

Living a life full of excellence is not difficult. Simply decide now to give it your best shot.

**Go the extra mile – and remember that there is no traffic jam on the extra mile.**

## Power Actions to Strive for Excellence Always

Write down five things at which you are already excellent. How can you get even better at these?

1. . . . . . . . . . . . . . . . . . . . . . . . . . . . . . . . . . . . . . . . . . . . .
. . . . . . . . . . . . . . . . . . . . . . . . . . . . . . . . . . . . . . . . . . . .

2. . . . . . . . . . . . . . . . . . . . . . . . . . . . . . . . . . . . . . . . . . . . .
. . . . . . . . . . . . . . . . . . . . . . . . . . . . . . . . . . . . . . . . . . . .

3. . . . . . . . . . . . . . . . . . . . . . . . . . . . . . . . . . . . . . . . . . . . .
. . . . . . . . . . . . . . . . . . . . . . . . . . . . . . . . . . . . . . . . . . . .

4. . . . . . . . . . . . . . . . . . . . . . . . . . . . . . . . . . . . . . . . . . . . .
. . . . . . . . . . . . . . . . . . . . . . . . . . . . . . . . . . . . . . . . . . . .

5. . . . . . . . . . . . . . . . . . . . . . . . . . . . . . . . . . . . . . . . . . . . .
. . . . . . . . . . . . . . . . . . . . . . . . . . . . . . . . . . . . . . . . . . . .

Write down five things you will do over the next seven days, to give people more than they expect.

1. . . . . . . . . . . . . . . . . . . . . . . . . . . . . . . . . . . . . . . . . . . . .
. . . . . . . . . . . . . . . . . . . . . . . . . . . . . . . . . . . . . . . . . . . .

2. . . . . . . . . . . . . . . . . . . . . . . . . . . . . . . . . . . . . . . . . . . . .
. . . . . . . . . . . . . . . . . . . . . . . . . . . . . . . . . . . . . . . . . . . .

3. . . . . . . . . . . . . . . . . . . . . . . . . . . . . . . . . . . . . . . . . . . . .
. . . . . . . . . . . . . . . . . . . . . . . . . . . . . . . . . . . . . . . . . . . .

4. . . . . . . . . . . . . . . . . . . . . . . . . . . . . . . . . . . . . . . . . . . . .
. . . . . . . . . . . . . . . . . . . . . . . . . . . . . . . . . . . . . . . . . . . .

5. . . . . . . . . . . . . . . . . . . . . . . . . . . . . . . . . . . . . . . . . . . . .
. . . . . . . . . . . . . . . . . . . . . . . . . . . . . . . . . . . . . . . . . . . .

Think of other areas in your life where you would like to develop excellence.

. . . . . . . . . . . . . . . . . . . . . . . . . . . . . . . . . . . . . . . . . . . . . . .

. . . . . . . . . . . . . . . . . . . . . . . . . . . . . . . . . . . . . . . . . . . . . . .

. . . . . . . . . . . . . . . . . . . . . . . . . . . . . . . . . . . . . . . . . . . . . . .

. . . . . . . . . . . . . . . . . . . . . . . . . . . . . . . . . . . . . . . . . . . . . . .

. . . . . . . . . . . . . . . . . . . . . . . . . . . . . . . . . . . . . . . . . . . . . . .

. . . . . . . . . . . . . . . . . . . . . . . . . . . . . . . . . . . . . . . . . . . . . . .

. . . . . . . . . . . . . . . . . . . . . . . . . . . . . . . . . . . . . . . . . . . . . . .

List five things you will do over the next fourteen days, to develop excellence in these areas.

1. . . . . . . . . . . . . . . . . . . . . . . . . . . . . . . . . . . . . . . . . . . . .

. . . . . . . . . . . . . . . . . . . . . . . . . . . . . . . . . . . . . . . . . . . . .

. . . . . . . . . . . . . . . . . . . . . . . . . . . . . . . . . . . . . . . . . . . . .

2. . . . . . . . . . . . . . . . . . . . . . . . . . . . . . . . . . . . . . . . . . . . .

. . . . . . . . . . . . . . . . . . . . . . . . . . . . . . . . . . . . . . . . . . . . .

. . . . . . . . . . . . . . . . . . . . . . . . . . . . . . . . . . . . . . . . . . . . .

3. . . . . . . . . . . . . . . . . . . . . . . . . . . . . . . . . . . . . . . . . . . . .

. . . . . . . . . . . . . . . . . . . . . . . . . . . . . . . . . . . . . . . . . . . . .

. . . . . . . . . . . . . . . . . . . . . . . . . . . . . . . . . . . . . . . . . . . . .

4. . . . . . . . . . . . . . . . . . . . . . . . . . . . . . . . . . . . . . . . . . . . .

. . . . . . . . . . . . . . . . . . . . . . . . . . . . . . . . . . . . . . . . . . . . .

. . . . . . . . . . . . . . . . . . . . . . . . . . . . . . . . . . . . . . . . . . . . .

5. . . . . . . . . . . . . . . . . . . . . . . . . . . . . . . . . . . . . . . . . . . . .

. . . . . . . . . . . . . . . . . . . . . . . . . . . . . . . . . . . . . . . . . . . . .

. . . . . . . . . . . . . . . . . . . . . . . . . . . . . . . . . . . . . . . . . . . . .

# 14 - GET INTO ACTION NOW

**O**nce you know what you want to create in your life, you will want to get started on it sooner rather than later.

Whatever you wish to accomplish, start right now. Action gets you where you want to go, whereas excuses hold you back. The choice is clearly yours. What are you waiting for to get started?

When you put things off, you waste a lot of time and energy worrying about them. When you are truly committed to reaching a set goal, there will always be something that can be done right away – so start on that right now.

When I wrote the first edition of this book, the whole process took just five weeks from the time I had the idea for the book to the defining moment when I had a hard copy in my hands. I was determined to write and publish the book, no matter what, and for those five weeks I was unstoppable. I had a clear goal, total focus, and the determination to keep going despite the late nights and endless revisions.

My friends who know me well have described me as 'unstoppable', once I have got focussed and my intent is clear about what I want to do. I get into a mode of relentless action until the task is done. The challenge for me now is to get that level of clarity more often before I get into action, rather than just jumping into action without a clear plan.

Ask yourself – what am I procrastinating about? Make a list of everything that you can think of, identify the most unpleasant job on your to do list and get stuck into it first before you do anything else. This will give you a great psychological boost and set you up for success. Everything else will seem easy.

When faced with a large or difficult task, break it down into small chunks and allocate 10 to 15 minutes to it every day. Then chip away steadily and soon you will feel that you are making progress.

By putting off the difficult tasks until the end of the day or the end of the week, you are simply allowing them to become more daunting. Remember you don't want to spend your weekends catching up.

**Also ask yourself what tasks you can give up that are not necessarily helping you towards creating the life you want.**

To get really motivated for action, reflect on what it's costing you to put things off. You are simply building up a lot of future pain and stress by not doing it now. Just feel that pain! Then imagine your rosier future if the task were to be completed now. Visualise how great you will feel once you have completed a task you've been putting off for a long time.

Tell yourself that you deserve better. Grit your teeth and become determined to have a procrastination-free life – you are worth it.

Plan your time and at the end of each day, plan the next day. If you have a to-do list, then include long term projects as well as the more imminent things that need doing. Consider having a will-do list too – a realistic but stretching list of things you must get done by the end of the day or the end of the week.

Prioritise your to-do list and do the most important things first. Do not let less important but easier tasks get in the way of that key action. Review this list, decide which tasks are no longer important and drop them.

Tackle the toughest task first. Start this at the beginning of the day or when your energy is highest. Be accountable for completing your tasks to another person who is interested in your success. Choose someone who won't be critical if you happen to fall short of your plans for the day.

Be selfish for a while and demand what you need, so as to create some breathing space in your life. Use this initial reserve of time to eliminate those things you have been procrastinating about.

Keep the decks clear once you have cleared all outstanding tasks. Take care of a task before it gets on a procrastination list. Sort your morning post immediately in one go: open it, file it, act on it, or dump it there and then.

Always remember my '3D' rule – do it, dump it or delegate and as a golden rule, never handle a piece of paper twice.

Deal with your emails ruthlessly and set aside fixed times of the day to deal with them. Unsubscribe from everything that no longer serves or interests you.

Take care of yourself and look after your health. This is key as sometimes we procrastinate simply because we are just too tired to take on another thing. Have an early night at least once a week, with ideally eight hours of sleep.

Reward yourself. Pat yourself on the back when you finish any task, especially something that you saw as difficult or challenging, and one that had been put off for a while.

Choose a personal reward that truly does it for you and something that will encourage you to tackle even more of those outstanding tasks. Maybe a massage, a trip to the theatre, a long luxurious candlelit bath, a trip into the countryside, a visit to a gallery or museum, or maybe just a stroll through the local park.

**Getting the important things done well and on time and cultivating a habit of being action-orientated will help you rapidly create the life you love.**

## Power Actions to Get into Action Now

List five things you have been putting off. Write a realistic date against each one, by when you will start to work on it.

Task                                    Date

1.  . . . . . . . . . . . . . . . . . . . . . . . . . . . . .     . . . . . . . . . . . . . . . . . . . . . . . . . . . .

2.  . . . . . . . . . . . . . . . . . . . . . . . . . . . . .     . . . . . . . . . . . . . . . . . . . . . . . . . . . .

3.  . . . . . . . . . . . . . . . . . . . . . . . . . . . . .     . . . . . . . . . . . . . . . . . . . . . . . . . . . .

4.  . . . . . . . . . . . . . . . . . . . . . . . . . . . . .     . . . . . . . . . . . . . . . . . . . . . . . . . . . .

5.  . . . . . . . . . . . . . . . . . . . . . . . . . . . . .     . . . . . . . . . . . . . . . . . . . . . . . . . . . .

Now, choose the task you will start on first. Write down here how great you felt when you started this task, and also when you finished it.

. . . . . . . . . . . . . . . . . . . . . . . . . . . . . . . . . . . . . . . . . . . . . . . . . . . .

. . . . . . . . . . . . . . . . . . . . . . . . . . . . . . . . . . . . . . . . . . . . . . . . . . . .

. . . . . . . . . . . . . . . . . . . . . . . . . . . . . . . . . . . . . . . . . . . . . . . . . . . .

. . . . . . . . . . . . . . . . . . . . . . . . . . . . . . . . . . . . . . . . . . . . . . . . . . . .

. . . . . . . . . . . . . . . . . . . . . . . . . . . . . . . . . . . . . . . . . . . . . . . . . . . .

. . . . . . . . . . . . . . . . . . . . . . . . . . . . . . . . . . . . . . . . . . . . . . . . . . . .

. . . . . . . . . . . . . . . . . . . . . . . . . . . . . . . . . . . . . . . . . . . . . . . . . . . .

List five things you can give up over the next seven days, things that will stop wasting your time. *For example, mindlessly surfing social media, collecting paperwork, storing newspapers, gossiping with office colleagues.*

1.  . . . . . . . . . . . . . . . . . . . . . . . . . . . . . . . . . . . . . . . . . . . . . . . .

2.  . . . . . . . . . . . . . . . . . . . . . . . . . . . . . . . . . . . . . . . . . . . . . . . .

3.  . . . . . . . . . . . . . . . . . . . . . . . . . . . . . . . . . . . . . . . . . . . . . . . .

4.  . . . . . . . . . . . . . . . . . . . . . . . . . . . . . . . . . . . . . . . . . . . . . . . .

5.  . . . . . . . . . . . . . . . . . . . . . . . . . . . . . . . . . . . . . . . . . . . . . . . .

List up to 10 things that you can do differently from this week onwards to make you more efficient and effective. *For example, check your emails less frequently, substitute phone calls for emails and plan the next day.*

1. .............................................................

2. .............................................................

3. .............................................................

4. .............................................................

5. .............................................................

6. .............................................................

7. .............................................................

8. .............................................................

9. .............................................................

10. .............................................................


Review your To-Do list. Which ones can you drop right now?

Challenge yourself to let go of at least 5 things. Cross these things out and let go of them right now.

.............................................................
.............................................................
.............................................................
.............................................................
.............................................................
.............................................................
.............................................................
.............................................................
.............................................................
.............................................................

# 15 - ENJOY THE WORK YOU DO NOW

**A**s you create the life you love and you live it, you want to function at your best, and to do work that you love.

After many years of being in jobs that I did not enjoy, I feel that I have now found what I am meant to be doing. When I came across coaching as a career a few years ago, it felt like coming home.

The work I do and enjoy now allows me to fully use all my skills and talents, and it fulfils my purpose of living a life of contribution. I also get the time and opportunity to connect with amazing people from many backgrounds.

**Do you love the work you do? Or would you rather be doing something else?**

No matter how good things are in other parts of your life such as family, social life and relationships, work is a major part of your life, and you can't afford to neglect it.

In the short term, whilst you may not be able to change jobs easily, you can certainly enjoy your work more. If you are not enjoying your current work, ask yourself if it is the job or if it is you. And reflect on what you can do to make your current work more enjoyable.

Remember that YOU are responsible for your life and if you cannot immediately change the job you are in, then it is up to you to make the most of it by approaching it with a more positive attitude.

When I used to work for a bank, I really did not like the job – I found the environment rather bureaucratic, and I felt stifled. I only looked forward to going into work on days when I had a squash match arranged during my lunch period. I was a different person on those days, I was motivated and eager.

On your way to work today, get yourself motivated to face the day. Think of how your job enables you to have your life outside of it. A positive attitude will make your day at work more pleasant and productive.

I realised within a few months that the job was not right for me, but it was another six years before I finally took the plunge and left. I made my experience at the bank more enjoyable by building a social life around my job and made some great friends. I also became active in the bank's social and cultural activities, and I feel I made a significant contribution towards improving morale in my department during a downturn period. I generally contributed towards creating a pleasant work environment despite the aggressive and stressful work ethos.

My time at the bank taught me a lot about corporate life and I bring a lot of that experience into my current work around coaching in the corporate world.

Things always turn out well for me – the bank made me redundant and offered me a reasonable severance package the very same week that I got accepted at business school for my MBA.

**Always expect things to turn out well for you.**

Keep your work in perspective and do the best you can in each situation. Consider the bigger picture. Do some voluntary work to gain a broader outlook.

Review what you can do to perform even better at your work. Ask what new resources and skills would help you. By adopting the Japanese approach of Kaizen of on-going improvement, you can cultivate a different, more empowering attitude towards your work.

When I worked at the bank, the resources of the organisation meant I was eligible to go on various training programmes and I made sure I fully benefited from my annual quota of training days. Every training opportunity you are offered is worth taking up. Though you may not see its immediate relevance for you, it is part of adding to your skills and it is often surprising how further down the road it turns out to be useful.

**Remember that you are far more than your work.**

Give up thinking that your work life 'should' be a certain way. Ask yourself: Who set these expectations in the first place? Parents? Teachers?

Concentrate on the task at hand and stay in the moment. Don't lose energy worrying about the undesirable situation you find yourself in. Plan your time, prioritise your to-do list, and do the most important things first. When performing any task, ask yourself if it is the best use of your time. Ruthlessly finish a task before it creeps on to a possible procrastination list. For example, if working in an office, sort out your incoming mail immediately in one go – open it, file, act on it or bin it there and then. Train yourself to do the same with incoming emails – stay on top of your inbox.

Delegate as much as possible Decide if there is anything that can be delegated, or that more fairly belongs to someone else's workload. Remember again my '3D' rule – do it, dump it or delegate and as a golden rule, never handle a piece of paper twice.

Have regular breaks and get away from your normal workplace, even if only for five minutes. For example, if working in an office environment, take a break from the computer, respond to emails only at set times during the day, and do leave your phone behind if it is not essential. Use your lunchtime for food, fresh air, and a mental break. Make sure you eat a healthy lunch and if you like to snack, make that healthy too – fruit rather than crisps or chocolate bars.

Contribute towards creating a pleasant work environment. Don't gossip – it just creates negativity all around. Have more fun at work, laugh more and chill out.

Review your day before you leave for home and look at what worked well, and what could be improved the next day. Switch off once you leave work and mentally say goodbye to your workspace the moment you leave for home. Don't take work home!

If you are mainly working from home, create strict boundaries around your times of working and have a separate office area if that's feasible for you.

Reward yourself at the end of your working day – you deserve it.

**See your work as a game. Life is meant to be fun – and if you are going to spend a third of it at work, you might as well enjoy it.**

## Power Actions to Enjoy the Work you Do Now

Write down up to five things that your current job allows you to have in your life.

1. ...............................................................

   ...............................................................

2. ...............................................................

   ...............................................................

3. ...............................................................

   ...............................................................

4. ...............................................................

   ...............................................................

5. ...............................................................

   ...............................................................

Make a list of up to five areas of your work that you currently don't enjoy. Next to each one, write down what you can do to develop each area, over the coming weeks, to make it more enjoyable.

| | Don't enjoy | How to make it more enjoyable |
|---|---|---|
| 1. | ............................ | ........................................ |
| | ............................ | ........................................ |
| 2. | ............................ | ........................................ |
| | ............................ | ........................................ |
| 3. | ............................ | ........................................ |
| | ............................ | ........................................ |
| 4. | ............................ | ........................................ |
| | ............................ | ........................................ |
| 5. | ............................ | ........................................ |
| | ............................ | ........................................ |

Write down five things you will do over the next fourteen days, to make your current job more enjoyable.

1. . . . . . . . . . . . . . . . . . . . . . . . . . . . . . . . . . . . . . . . . . . . . . . . . . . . .

. . . . . . . . . . . . . . . . . . . . . . . . . . . . . . . . . . . . . . . . . . . . . . . . . . . .

2. . . . . . . . . . . . . . . . . . . . . . . . . . . . . . . . . . . . . . . . . . . . . . . . . . . . .

. . . . . . . . . . . . . . . . . . . . . . . . . . . . . . . . . . . . . . . . . . . . . . . . . . . .

3. . . . . . . . . . . . . . . . . . . . . . . . . . . . . . . . . . . . . . . . . . . . . . . . . . . . .

. . . . . . . . . . . . . . . . . . . . . . . . . . . . . . . . . . . . . . . . . . . . . . . . . . . .

4. . . . . . . . . . . . . . . . . . . . . . . . . . . . . . . . . . . . . . . . . . . . . . . . . . . . .

. . . . . . . . . . . . . . . . . . . . . . . . . . . . . . . . . . . . . . . . . . . . . . . . . . . .

5. . . . . . . . . . . . . . . . . . . . . . . . . . . . . . . . . . . . . . . . . . . . . . . . . . . . .

. . . . . . . . . . . . . . . . . . . . . . . . . . . . . . . . . . . . . . . . . . . . . . . . . . . .


List five resources or skills that would help you perform even better at work.

1. . . . . . . . . . . . . . . . . . . . . . . . . . . . . . . . . . . . . . . . . . . . . . . . . . . . .

2. . . . . . . . . . . . . . . . . . . . . . . . . . . . . . . . . . . . . . . . . . . . . . . . . . . . .

3. . . . . . . . . . . . . . . . . . . . . . . . . . . . . . . . . . . . . . . . . . . . . . . . . . . . .

4. . . . . . . . . . . . . . . . . . . . . . . . . . . . . . . . . . . . . . . . . . . . . . . . . . . . .

5. . . . . . . . . . . . . . . . . . . . . . . . . . . . . . . . . . . . . . . . . . . . . . . . . . . . .

How can you get these resources or develop these skills?

1. . . . . . . . . . . . . . . . . . . . . . . . . . . . . . . . . . . . . . . . . . . . . . . . . . . . .

2. . . . . . . . . . . . . . . . . . . . . . . . . . . . . . . . . . . . . . . . . . . . . . . . . . . . .

3. . . . . . . . . . . . . . . . . . . . . . . . . . . . . . . . . . . . . . . . . . . . . . . . . . . . .

4. . . . . . . . . . . . . . . . . . . . . . . . . . . . . . . . . . . . . . . . . . . . . . . . . . . . .

5. . . . . . . . . . . . . . . . . . . . . . . . . . . . . . . . . . . . . . . . . . . . . . . . . . . . .

## 16 – FIND THE WORK YOU LOVE

An essential part of creating the life you love is to find work you will love and enjoy doing.

When you find such work, you will proverbially jump out of bed looking forward to the day and the adventures to come.

If you do not love your work and you would rather be doing something else, then you have the responsibility for changing it. When I worked at the bank, I was really fed up and got so disillusioned with the world of computers that I decided to take a career break and go to business school to broaden my skills. I took a huge risk as this meant no income for a year and living on my savings.

People are either unsure about what they really do want to do, apathetic about finding what they really love doing or are simply resigned to being in this situation.

When I went to business school, I was still not sure about what I wanted to do beyond the course, but I knew that the studies I undertook would open many new doors for opportunity and would lead to new connections. As it happened, years later, I ended up joining a dot.com Internet start-up company that was established by a friend I met on my business course.

**You never know what is around the corner or in the not-too-distant future.**

Do you love the work that you do, or would you rather be doing something else? Ask yourself if the payoff you get financially, or in any other way, is worth being in the wrong job with the potential for years of resentment and drudgery.

In the short term you can do a lot to begin enjoying the job that you do. In the medium to long term, almost anyone can find a job that they enjoy – it may take time and perseverance, but it can be done. No matter how good things are in other parts of your life such as family, social life, and relationships, it would be a shame if the work part of your life were to be compromised or neglected.

So do not wait to be rescued – there is no second chance in life. This is it – go out and find the job that you really crave for. It is YOUR situation, and you have the responsibility for changing it. Think about your gains and reflect on how you would feel in the years to come if you do not give yourself a chance now to find and do the work you really want.

Ask yourself if your current job has now become something different from what it was when you first started it. If so, would you still choose this job if offered to you again today? If the answer is no, then start looking around – update that CV or résumé and start planning your job search.

Remember that it is your life, and you always have a choice in what you do, where you work and for whom. You once chose to do the job you have now, even though at the time, you may not even have been conscious of making this choice.

Are you living someone else's life? If you are a lawyer, is there a painter impatiently trying to emerge? Or if you are a builder, perhaps you have always wanted to be a writer or a computer whiz-kid?

**Ask yourself: What do I really want?**

Look at your core values and base your work around them. If necessary, review your values and see if they have changed. Once the work is based around the foundation of your values, it will become joyful, energising, fulfilling and almost effortless. Ensure that your work nurtures such values as creativity, integrity, and a desire to contribute. Otherwise, you will naturally feel frustrated and bored, and you may have a nagging feeling that something is missing.

Connect with your passion. What is it that when you do it, you lose all track of time and awareness? Consider what you would do if you had all the time and money in the world. Reflect on what things really make you buzz and what contribution you want to make to the world. Get clear about what you want to be remembered for.

**What unique talents do you have to offer the world?**

Stop following other people's dreams. Ask yourself why you are doing what you do right now. Is it something that someone said 'you should be doing' or did you take on this job or career because of peer pressure? Maybe this was what your parents and teachers expected you to do.

It took me many years to realise that I had continued working for a bank purely because it was seen to be a prestigious thing to do, and my parents were proud of where I worked. This was the same reason I worked for a major petroleum company. I accepted the job partly because I knew I would be the envy of my college friends as it was a prestigious position – but in both instances, I quickly knew that I was in the wrong place.

Even if you can't just jump into the job you would like, you can still get satisfaction in other ways. For example, say you want to be a film actor. It is unlikely you will earn a living at it from day one, so it could be risky to give up the job you have. You could though work your dream into your daily life by taking acting classes in your spare time and auditioning for short films just to get more experience.

Once you are in a job that you love, there will be so many positives. You will look forward to each day and feel that you are leading a life that counts. Your self-esteem will increase, and you will feel and look great. You will be buzzing, and people will find that it is fun to have you around them.

Focus on your long-term gains from changing jobs – most change is confronting, and it takes courage. If you feel you would have a lot to lose by giving up an established job, then look at all the positive things that can happen from the change.

Get into action. Once you have decided that you want change, don't let laziness, negative feelings or other people hold you back. Acknowledge that there are some obstacles in your way, and then begin to tackle them. Do something right away, such as applying online, making a phone call, or sending an email. The energy for change will begin to build from this one single act.

**Finding work you love and enjoy will go a long way to creating and living the life you love.**

## Power Actions to Find the Work you Love

Sit down quietly and visualise yourself doing your dream work. Where are you? Who are you with? What are you doing? Now, write down the first 10 words or phrases that come into your mind.

1. . . . . . . . . . . . . . . . . . . . . . . . . . . . . . . . . . . . . . . . . . . . . . . . . . . . .

2. . . . . . . . . . . . . . . . . . . . . . . . . . . . . . . . . . . . . . . . . . . . . . . . . . . . .

3. . . . . . . . . . . . . . . . . . . . . . . . . . . . . . . . . . . . . . . . . . . . . . . . . . . . .

4. . . . . . . . . . . . . . . . . . . . . . . . . . . . . . . . . . . . . . . . . . . . . . . . . . . . .

5. . . . . . . . . . . . . . . . . . . . . . . . . . . . . . . . . . . . . . . . . . . . . . . . . . . . .

6. . . . . . . . . . . . . . . . . . . . . . . . . . . . . . . . . . . . . . . . . . . . . . . . . . . . .

7. . . . . . . . . . . . . . . . . . . . . . . . . . . . . . . . . . . . . . . . . . . . . . . . . . . . .

8. . . . . . . . . . . . . . . . . . . . . . . . . . . . . . . . . . . . . . . . . . . . . . . . . . . . .

9. . . . . . . . . . . . . . . . . . . . . . . . . . . . . . . . . . . . . . . . . . . . . . . . . . . . .

10. . . . . . . . . . . . . . . . . . . . . . . . . . . . . . . . . . . . . . . . . . . . . . . . . . . . .

Write down any other ideas or thoughts that might have come to you.

. . . . . . . . . . . . . . . . . . . . . . . . . . . . . . . . . . . . . . . . . . . . . . . . . . . . . .

. . . . . . . . . . . . . . . . . . . . . . . . . . . . . . . . . . . . . . . . . . . . . . . . . . . . . .

. . . . . . . . . . . . . . . . . . . . . . . . . . . . . . . . . . . . . . . . . . . . . . . . . . . . . .

. . . . . . . . . . . . . . . . . . . . . . . . . . . . . . . . . . . . . . . . . . . . . . . . . . . . . .

. . . . . . . . . . . . . . . . . . . . . . . . . . . . . . . . . . . . . . . . . . . . . . . . . . . . . .

. . . . . . . . . . . . . . . . . . . . . . . . . . . . . . . . . . . . . . . . . . . . . . . . . . . . . .

. . . . . . . . . . . . . . . . . . . . . . . . . . . . . . . . . . . . . . . . . . . . . . . . . . . . . .

. . . . . . . . . . . . . . . . . . . . . . . . . . . . . . . . . . . . . . . . . . . . . . . . . . . . . .

. . . . . . . . . . . . . . . . . . . . . . . . . . . . . . . . . . . . . . . . . . . . . . . . . . . . . .

. . . . . . . . . . . . . . . . . . . . . . . . . . . . . . . . . . . . . . . . . . . . . . . . . . . . . .

. . . . . . . . . . . . . . . . . . . . . . . . . . . . . . . . . . . . . . . . . . . . . . . . . . . . . .

. . . . . . . . . . . . . . . . . . . . . . . . . . . . . . . . . . . . . . . . . . . . . . . . . . . . . .

. . . . . . . . . . . . . . . . . . . . . . . . . . . . . . . . . . . . . . . . . . . . . . . . . . . . . .

Write down at least five things that you would rather be doing as your work instead of what you currently do.

1. . . . . . . . . . . . . . . . . . . . . . . . . . . . . . . . . . . . . . . . . . . . . . . . . . . . . . . . .

2. . . . . . . . . . . . . . . . . . . . . . . . . . . . . . . . . . . . . . . . . . . . . . . . . . . . . . . . .

3. . . . . . . . . . . . . . . . . . . . . . . . . . . . . . . . . . . . . . . . . . . . . . . . . . . . . . . . .

4. . . . . . . . . . . . . . . . . . . . . . . . . . . . . . . . . . . . . . . . . . . . . . . . . . . . . . . . .

5. . . . . . . . . . . . . . . . . . . . . . . . . . . . . . . . . . . . . . . . . . . . . . . . . . . . . . . . .

List up to five things you would gain by changing your current work.

1. . . . . . . . . . . . . . . . . . . . . . . . . . . . . . . . . . . . . . . . . . . . . . . . . . . . . . . . .

2. . . . . . . . . . . . . . . . . . . . . . . . . . . . . . . . . . . . . . . . . . . . . . . . . . . . . . . . .

3. . . . . . . . . . . . . . . . . . . . . . . . . . . . . . . . . . . . . . . . . . . . . . . . . . . . . . . . .

4. . . . . . . . . . . . . . . . . . . . . . . . . . . . . . . . . . . . . . . . . . . . . . . . . . . . . . . . .

5. . . . . . . . . . . . . . . . . . . . . . . . . . . . . . . . . . . . . . . . . . . . . . . . . . . . . . . . .

List three things you will do over the next seven days, to move towards your dream work.

1. . . . . . . . . . . . . . . . . . . . . . . . . . . . . . . . . . . . . . . . . . . . . . . . . . . . . . . . .

. . . . . . . . . . . . . . . . . . . . . . . . . . . . . . . . . . . . . . . . . . . . . . . . . . . . . . . .

. . . . . . . . . . . . . . . . . . . . . . . . . . . . . . . . . . . . . . . . . . . . . . . . . . . . . . . .

2. . . . . . . . . . . . . . . . . . . . . . . . . . . . . . . . . . . . . . . . . . . . . . . . . . . . . . . . .

. . . . . . . . . . . . . . . . . . . . . . . . . . . . . . . . . . . . . . . . . . . . . . . . . . . . . . . .

. . . . . . . . . . . . . . . . . . . . . . . . . . . . . . . . . . . . . . . . . . . . . . . . . . . . . . . .

3. . . . . . . . . . . . . . . . . . . . . . . . . . . . . . . . . . . . . . . . . . . . . . . . . . . . . . . . .

. . . . . . . . . . . . . . . . . . . . . . . . . . . . . . . . . . . . . . . . . . . . . . . . . . . . . . . .

. . . . . . . . . . . . . . . . . . . . . . . . . . . . . . . . . . . . . . . . . . . . . . . . . . . . . . . .

# 17 – CREATE WORK-LIFE BALANCE

To create and live the life you love, you must have balance in your life, with enough time spent with your loved ones. You also want to have enough resources and activities to make your life enjoyable and fun.

Your best life is like a precious tapestry – it becomes magical when all the various bits weave together well.

A few years ago, when I was in the process of becoming a dot.com paper millionaire and then losing it all, I worked crazy 20-hour days non-stop for nine months. In that time, though it was all very exhilarating, the cost to me was poor health, no other life, and a strained marriage. Ultimately, my marriage ended, though of course my involvement with the dot.com company was not the only factor. It became clear how little time we had spent with each other over the previous years and how out of balance our lives had become.

Just how do you learn to lead a balanced and yet full life? So many people are working so hard that they seem to have lost sight of the reason for working in the first place. I work quite hard now as a coach, and I know the reason I do so is it gives me so much fulfilment, deep connections with people and brings me new opportunities every day.

Not everyone has the luxury of being able to quit their job – but you can certainly make a choice today of how best to balance your life between your own downtime, your family, and your work.

As far as I know, no one on their deathbed has ever wished that they had worked harder and spent more time in the office. Their regrets are usually about not spending enough time with their loved ones and not having done everything they wanted to do in their lifetime.

Connect with the real reason why you work extra hours each week. Ask yourself if there is a good reason for this? How is it serving you? If the answer is that it is something you need to do because you need the extra money, or the project is crucial for your company, client, or customer, then that is ample justification.

However, is the real reason you are working so hard and long because you feel you should, since everyone else does too? If you have got into that habit, then ask yourself if you can do things differently. What can you do to become more productive in fewer hours?

Perhaps where you work is a very structured, hierarchical company which makes it hard for you to do things differently. Peer pressure and management expectations may mean that you are required to put in long hours or at least seen to be doing so. You certainly can make some changes, but if it is obvious that things will not change, it might be time to review the situation and ask yourself if this is what you really want in the long term.

Are you taking on too much at work? Trying to do everything yourself can be a huge waste of time and can keep you working much longer hours. Delegate, and learn to accept that even if the task isn't completed to your own high standards, it is okay if it's been done well enough. Remember the 80/20 rule, whereby 80% of any benefit or result of a task comes from the first 20% of effort. Most people spend 80% of their energies on perfecting the last 20% when it is not necessary.

Do you work to live, or live to work? If you feel you are working overtly hard, ask yourself if you are hiding from something. Ask if you are truly happy with yourself, with your life, and with your family. Or perhaps you are so unhappy that you find a refuge by drowning in paperwork or whatever else you deal with at work.

Do not bring work home. Have a clear boundary between work and personal life. If you work from home, have clear cut boundaries between when you start and finish working – no checking emails late at night for example.

**Allow time daily for quality moments with your partner, family, and friends.**

Make this action a priority every day. If you have children, spend as much time with them as you can. If you only get home to spend the half hour before bedtime with them, then make sure you have time available at the weekend as a priority.

Have regular holidays or even a weekend or day away on a regular basis. It is important that you are spending time with your loved ones so make the time for a break with them. Spend quality time with a few select friends, those who energise and uplift you.

Weekends are for recharging your batteries. Plan something relaxing and rejuvenating with the family. Plan your weekends as a treat for yourself. After allowing time for domestic chores, make the maximum time available to spend with family or friends.

Relax daily and not just on Friday evenings or when you feel you deserve it. Focus on relaxing before your day starts, when stuck in traffic, or when faced with any issue or challenge. Make relaxation a state of mind, rather than something you reward yourself with at the end of the day or week.

Take some time out for yourself daily and get some stillness. This could be something as simple as putting your feet up for 15 minutes.

Explore ways of bringing more stillness and quiet time in your life such as meditation, early morning walks in the park, listening to soothing music, or reading a good book.

**Your loved ones will benefit from you being more grounded, and you will thrive too. Live the life you love around your family and friends, and not the other way around.**

## Power Actions to Create Work-Life Balance

Think of up to five reasons why you are currently working so hard.

1. . . . . . . . . . . . . . . . . . . . . . . . . . . . . . . . . . . . . . . . . . . . . . . . . . . . . .

   . . . . . . . . . . . . . . . . . . . . . . . . . . . . . . . . . . . . . . . . . . . . . . . . . . . . .

2. . . . . . . . . . . . . . . . . . . . . . . . . . . . . . . . . . . . . . . . . . . . . . . . . . . . . .

   . . . . . . . . . . . . . . . . . . . . . . . . . . . . . . . . . . . . . . . . . . . . . . . . . . . . .

3. . . . . . . . . . . . . . . . . . . . . . . . . . . . . . . . . . . . . . . . . . . . . . . . . . . . . .

   . . . . . . . . . . . . . . . . . . . . . . . . . . . . . . . . . . . . . . . . . . . . . . . . . . . . .

4. . . . . . . . . . . . . . . . . . . . . . . . . . . . . . . . . . . . . . . . . . . . . . . . . . . . . .

   . . . . . . . . . . . . . . . . . . . . . . . . . . . . . . . . . . . . . . . . . . . . . . . . . . . . .

5. . . . . . . . . . . . . . . . . . . . . . . . . . . . . . . . . . . . . . . . . . . . . . . . . . . . . .

   . . . . . . . . . . . . . . . . . . . . . . . . . . . . . . . . . . . . . . . . . . . . . . . . . . . . .

What is the cost to you of working so hard? Think about the impact on not just you but also those people around you. *For example, stress and other adverse effects on your health, loss of quality time with family, no social life.*

. . . . . . . . . . . . . . . . . . . . . . . . . . . . . . . . . . . . . . . . . . . . . . . . . . . . . . . . . . .

. . . . . . . . . . . . . . . . . . . . . . . . . . . . . . . . . . . . . . . . . . . . . . . . . . . . . . . . . . .

. . . . . . . . . . . . . . . . . . . . . . . . . . . . . . . . . . . . . . . . . . . . . . . . . . . . . . . . . . .

. . . . . . . . . . . . . . . . . . . . . . . . . . . . . . . . . . . . . . . . . . . . . . . . . . . . . . . . . . .

. . . . . . . . . . . . . . . . . . . . . . . . . . . . . . . . . . . . . . . . . . . . . . . . . . . . . . . . . . .

. . . . . . . . . . . . . . . . . . . . . . . . . . . . . . . . . . . . . . . . . . . . . . . . . . . . . . . . . . .

. . . . . . . . . . . . . . . . . . . . . . . . . . . . . . . . . . . . . . . . . . . . . . . . . . . . . . . . . . .

. . . . . . . . . . . . . . . . . . . . . . . . . . . . . . . . . . . . . . . . . . . . . . . . . . . . . . . . . . .

. . . . . . . . . . . . . . . . . . . . . . . . . . . . . . . . . . . . . . . . . . . . . . . . . . . . . . . . . . .

. . . . . . . . . . . . . . . . . . . . . . . . . . . . . . . . . . . . . . . . . . . . . . . . . . . . . . . . . . .

Think of three reasons for spending more time with your family or friends.

1. . . . . . . . . . . . . . . . . . . . . . . . . . . . . . . . . . . . . . . . . . . . . . . . . . . .

. . . . . . . . . . . . . . . . . . . . . . . . . . . . . . . . . . . . . . . . . . . . . . . . . . .

2. . . . . . . . . . . . . . . . . . . . . . . . . . . . . . . . . . . . . . . . . . . . . . . . . . . .

. . . . . . . . . . . . . . . . . . . . . . . . . . . . . . . . . . . . . . . . . . . . . . . . . . .

3. . . . . . . . . . . . . . . . . . . . . . . . . . . . . . . . . . . . . . . . . . . . . . . . . . . .

. . . . . . . . . . . . . . . . . . . . . . . . . . . . . . . . . . . . . . . . . . . . . . . . . . .

List five things that you will do in the next 14 days, to spend more time with your family or friends.

1. . . . . . . . . . . . . . . . . . . . . . . . . . . . . . . . . . . . . . . . . . . . . . . . . . . .

2. . . . . . . . . . . . . . . . . . . . . . . . . . . . . . . . . . . . . . . . . . . . . . . . . . . .

3. . . . . . . . . . . . . . . . . . . . . . . . . . . . . . . . . . . . . . . . . . . . . . . . . . . .

4. . . . . . . . . . . . . . . . . . . . . . . . . . . . . . . . . . . . . . . . . . . . . . . . . . . .

5. . . . . . . . . . . . . . . . . . . . . . . . . . . . . . . . . . . . . . . . . . . . . . . . . . . .

Think of five things you can do differently in your work life to become more productive in fewer hours.

1. . . . . . . . . . . . . . . . . . . . . . . . . . . . . . . . . . . . . . . . . . . . . . . . . . . .

. . . . . . . . . . . . . . . . . . . . . . . . . . . . . . . . . . . . . . . . . . . . . . . . . . .

2. . . . . . . . . . . . . . . . . . . . . . . . . . . . . . . . . . . . . . . . . . . . . . . . . . . .

. . . . . . . . . . . . . . . . . . . . . . . . . . . . . . . . . . . . . . . . . . . . . . . . . . .

3. . . . . . . . . . . . . . . . . . . . . . . . . . . . . . . . . . . . . . . . . . . . . . . . . . . .

. . . . . . . . . . . . . . . . . . . . . . . . . . . . . . . . . . . . . . . . . . . . . . . . . . .

4. . . . . . . . . . . . . . . . . . . . . . . . . . . . . . . . . . . . . . . . . . . . . . . . . . . .

. . . . . . . . . . . . . . . . . . . . . . . . . . . . . . . . . . . . . . . . . . . . . . . . . . .

5. . . . . . . . . . . . . . . . . . . . . . . . . . . . . . . . . . . . . . . . . . . . . . . . . . . .

. . . . . . . . . . . . . . . . . . . . . . . . . . . . . . . . . . . . . . . . . . . . . . . . . . .

## 18 – MANAGE YOUR MONEY

**To live the life you love, you need the financial resources to support you and your chosen lifestyle.**

Money is simply a means to an end, something that provides you with the energy to create your dreams. Ideally you want to be in control of your money, with financial reserves and a savings plan that will make you comfortable – not only now, but in the future too.

I was a dot.com paper millionaire around the turn of the millennium and when I visited India, I was feted as someone who had made it! And this was before any of the money had even been earned. This was a classic case of building castles in the air, and I was the builder.

Alas our dot.com venture collapsed as fast as it had risen and a lot of egos were bruised and quite a few paper fortunes had been earned, spent, and lost.

Looking back now, for a while I had become something that was not resonant with my values, and it was not really me – I had become greedy and arrogant. It was a blessing in disguise for me that the dot.com company collapsed. Years later, I now seek and desire financial freedom but in a manner that is in line with me and my values.

My definition of financial freedom is to be able to choose and do what I want around my work and at the same time have a standard of living that I desire. Money has always come easily to me. No matter what I have done, I have made money and my next goal is to become even better at investing it.

**To ultimately have financial freedom, get to know where you are now and where you want to go.**

Affirm to yourself that you are no longer going to put up with scarcity and money pressures in your life anymore.

Start being prudent with how you spend your money and begin to save and invest. After all, your financial situation is determined by how much you keep and not by how much you earn.

Plug your money drains and look at ways of cutting back your expenditure. For example, look at rationalising your utility bills.

Review any limiting beliefs you may have about money and ask where they came from. Learn from other people, to whom your limiting beliefs do not seem to apply. Replace those beliefs with positive affirmations such as 'money flows to me in abundance'.

Get your debts under control. The longer a situation such as this is ignored, the worse it gets. Somehow our Western culture makes us believe that we need everything new, we need it right now, and it is acceptable to incur debt - but being out of control with our finances can be such a burden.

Total up the exact amount of your debt. Include your mortgage, loans, and any other personal debts. Calculate your exact monthly income and your exact monthly expenditure. If you are self-employed or have a variable income, then see if you can work out an average income, based on the previous few months or on your own expectation of future income. Now work out a monthly repayment plan to reduce your debt and get expert advice if necessary.

Have a plan for saving every month, where you can put away, say, five per cent of your net earnings in a long-term savings account. Knowing that this is there and building up for you will give you a greater sense of security.

Make your money go a long way. Research the best places for deals and special offers – look online and get ideas from others via social media.

**Even better, ask yourself IF you really need to even buy the item in the first place.**

Educate yourself about money matters by looking at the many resources out there: online, books, courses, and seminars. Read the financial section of the daily papers. Where possible, use the resources of the local library and borrow books rather than buying them.

Check out what prominent financial experts in your country have to say about the current financial trends and ways of saving money. But of course, make your own decisions based on your own sense and situation.

Talk openly about money issues and learn from your contacts. Talking about money is still taboo for a lot of people and it is not considered polite to discuss money issues.

Decide for yourself when and what would be appropriate and look out for any hot tips such as where to get a good deal on mobile phones, electrical goods or even which shares to invest in. Of course, use your own judgement before making any decision.

Invest in your own self-development. Set aside, say, five per cent of your income towards training courses, events, seminars, phone apps, books and working with a coach. Be open to learning and investing in your own growth and development. This will ultimately help you create a better life, increase your earning potential – and help you to attain financial freedom.

**Developing financial discipline and prudence will help you go a long way towards building a solid foundation for creating and living a life you love.**

## Power Actions to Manage Your Money

List up to 10 ways in which you can immediately start saving money and cutting back on unnecessary expenditure.

1. . . . . . . . . . . . . . . . . . . . . . . . . . . . . . . . . . . . . . . . . . . . . . .

2. . . . . . . . . . . . . . . . . . . . . . . . . . . . . . . . . . . . . . . . . . . . . . .

3. . . . . . . . . . . . . . . . . . . . . . . . . . . . . . . . . . . . . . . . . . . . . . .

4. . . . . . . . . . . . . . . . . . . . . . . . . . . . . . . . . . . . . . . . . . . . . . .

5. . . . . . . . . . . . . . . . . . . . . . . . . . . . . . . . . . . . . . . . . . . . . . .

6. . . . . . . . . . . . . . . . . . . . . . . . . . . . . . . . . . . . . . . . . . . . . . .

7. . . . . . . . . . . . . . . . . . . . . . . . . . . . . . . . . . . . . . . . . . . . . . .

8. . . . . . . . . . . . . . . . . . . . . . . . . . . . . . . . . . . . . . . . . . . . . . .

9. . . . . . . . . . . . . . . . . . . . . . . . . . . . . . . . . . . . . . . . . . . . . . .

10. . . . . . . . . . . . . . . . . . . . . . . . . . . . . . . . . . . . . . . . . . . . . . .

List three limiting beliefs you have about money. What positive statements can you replace them with? *For example, if you currently believe that money is hard to come by, you can instead start saying "Money comes to me easily and in abundance".*

Belief 1 . . . . . . . . . . . . . . . . . . . . . . . . . . . . . . . . . . . . . . . . . . .

Positive statement 1 . . . . . . . . . . . . . . . . . . . . . . . . . . . . . . . . . . . . .

. . . . . . . . . . . . . . . . . . . . . . . . . . . . . . . . . . . . . . . . . . . . . . . .

Belief 2 . . . . . . . . . . . . . . . . . . . . . . . . . . . . . . . . . . . . . . . . . . .

Positive statement 2 . . . . . . . . . . . . . . . . . . . . . . . . . . . . . . . . . . . . .

. . . . . . . . . . . . . . . . . . . . . . . . . . . . . . . . . . . . . . . . . . . . . . . .

Belief 3 . . . . . . . . . . . . . . . . . . . . . . . . . . . . . . . . . . . . . . . . . . .

Positive statement 3 . . . . . . . . . . . . . . . . . . . . . . . . . . . . . . . . . . . . .

. . . . . . . . . . . . . . . . . . . . . . . . . . . . . . . . . . . . . . . . . . . . . . . .

List five things you will do over the next month, to educate yourself about money matters.

1. . . . . . . . . . . . . . . . . . . . . . . . . . . . . . . . . . . . . . . . . . . . . . . . .

2. . . . . . . . . . . . . . . . . . . . . . . . . . . . . . . . . . . . . . . . . . . . . . . . .

3. . . . . . . . . . . . . . . . . . . . . . . . . . . . . . . . . . . . . . . . . . . . . . . . .

4. . . . . . . . . . . . . . . . . . . . . . . . . . . . . . . . . . . . . . . . . . . . . . . . .

5. . . . . . . . . . . . . . . . . . . . . . . . . . . . . . . . . . . . . . . . . . . . . . . . .

Work out a monthly repayment plan to reduce your debt. (Do this by first reviewing all your debts. Then calculate your exact monthly income – estimate this if you are self-employed or have a variable income – and calculate your exact monthly expenditure.)

. . . . . . . . . . . . . . . . . . . . . . . . . . . . . . . . . . . . . . . . . . . . . . . . . . .

. . . . . . . . . . . . . . . . . . . . . . . . . . . . . . . . . . . . . . . . . . . . . . . . . . .

. . . . . . . . . . . . . . . . . . . . . . . . . . . . . . . . . . . . . . . . . . . . . . . . . . .

. . . . . . . . . . . . . . . . . . . . . . . . . . . . . . . . . . . . . . . . . . . . . . . . . . .

Brainstorm with a partner, trusted friend, or a coach 10 ways of increasing your income. Which ones will you start on and when?

1. . . . . . . . . . . . . . . . . . . . . . . . . . . . . . . . . . . . . . . . . . . . . . . . .

2. . . . . . . . . . . . . . . . . . . . . . . . . . . . . . . . . . . . . . . . . . . . . . . . .

3. . . . . . . . . . . . . . . . . . . . . . . . . . . . . . . . . . . . . . . . . . . . . . . . .

4. . . . . . . . . . . . . . . . . . . . . . . . . . . . . . . . . . . . . . . . . . . . . . . . .

5. . . . . . . . . . . . . . . . . . . . . . . . . . . . . . . . . . . . . . . . . . . . . . . . .

6. . . . . . . . . . . . . . . . . . . . . . . . . . . . . . . . . . . . . . . . . . . . . . . . .

7. . . . . . . . . . . . . . . . . . . . . . . . . . . . . . . . . . . . . . . . . . . . . . . . .

8. . . . . . . . . . . . . . . . . . . . . . . . . . . . . . . . . . . . . . . . . . . . . . . . .

9. . . . . . . . . . . . . . . . . . . . . . . . . . . . . . . . . . . . . . . . . . . . . . . . .

10. . . . . . . . . . . . . . . . . . . . . . . . . . . . . . . . . . . . . . . . . . . . . . . . .

# 19 – TAKE TOTAL SELF-CARE

To create the life you love and to continue to live it means that you must be fit and healthy to do so. How much self-care you take will make a huge difference to your life.

Your health and well-being are the foundation of your life. You can have all the money and time in the world, yet without good health they would be worthless.

The emphasis here is on 'total'– you must be willing to make major changes in all areas that are holding you back, including those long-established habits that no longer serve your best interests. You only have one body and today is the day to start taking care of it.

### What will you do to make your body a 'temple'?

I began to feel much healthier when I adopted a vegetarian diet a few years ago. Soon after, I gave up drinking copious amounts of coffee, tea, and alcohol, although I still enjoy the occasional celebratory glass of champagne. This is not to say that everyone should become a vegetarian – it is what suited me.

My health also improved rapidly when I found out my body was intolerant to milk, and I promptly gave it up. Today, my healthy eating and self-care habits, combined with lots of fresh air and early morning walks in the park, mean that I am now the healthiest I have ever been. Due to an old injury, I have had to stop playing my favourite sport squash as regularly as before. But that is an example of self-care too as I am listening to my body and heeding its advice.

Just imagine how much better your life would be in the years to come if you had optimum health. Conversely how much more fun and vibrant would your life be today, if you had taken better care of yourself years ago?

Ask yourself if you are seriously willing to start and commit to a regime of total self-care. Your body will thank you in the years to come. It absolutely relies on you to do the best for it – please do not let it down any longer.

The body is able and willing to heal itself of many physical conditions if you give it a chance. Begin to take total self-care today and you can soon see improvements in the damage inflicted by previous poor self-care.

Of course, not all conditions can be reversed or healed although most will see a significant improvement. I suffered a badly twisted ankle many years ago and this has inhibited me from playing squash to the competitive level I would like to. Through continual self-care, I know that this injury will not get any worse in the long term. Remember that whatever positive steps you take in looking after yourself will make a noticeable difference to you.

Drink lots of water. A minimum of two litres a day will make an immediate difference as toxins get flushed out of your body cells. If you are not used to drinking this amount, start slowly and build up. Have a glass of water for every other drink you have until you are drinking plain water every day.

Cut down on fried food, sugar, meat, and dairy products. Consider taking on a healthier lifestyle by having more fresh fruit and vegetables, whole-grains, and vegetarian food. On a balanced diet, you will also need fewer supplements.

Eat the best food you can, as if you eat junk food, your body will feel lethargic, tired and suffer in the long term. It is a cliché but so true – you are what you eat – so no more junk food. Also cut down on eating out – nothing beats fresh home-cooked food. Eat moderately, minimise snacking and wherever possible, eat organic food.

Breathe deeply and right down to your stomach. You will take in more air and benefit instantly as the extra oxygen makes your cells perk up, release toxins and function more efficiently.

**Exercise daily and make it fun and enjoyable.**

If the gym doesn't appeal to you, go for a daily walk, or take a dance class – find something that you enjoy and you will stick to it more easily. Remind yourself of the benefits and adopt exercise habits as part of your daily routine of total self-care. For example, take the stairs instead of the escalator or lift; and get off the bus a couple of stops early and walk to your destination. Or like me, get an indoor trampoline, which I find energising, uplifting and therapeutic.

Cut down on caffeine and consider gradually cutting it out completely. That means no coffee, black tea, cola, or chocolate! Instead have herbal and fruit teas - experiment with the many types and brands available to find one you really like. It takes only a few weeks to wean your body off caffeine – just make sure you drink plenty of water as it will help you eliminate it faster. As your body begins to cleanse itself, you may experience some short-term discomfort such as headaches or irritability.

Cut out cigarettes, as smoking has no place in your regime of total self-care. If you need help to give up, there are various sources of help you can get. Just find the approach that works for you. If you are determined, you could give up today but a swift stop to smoking does not work for everyone. You may be better off cutting down gradually and using patches or other methods to support you. Whatever method you choose, go gently on yourself, and know that once you are determined and committed to give up, you will do so sooner rather than later.

Reduce your alcohol intake and drink more water instead. Consider cutting down on alcohol as excessive drinking is linked to numerous health risks such as heart disease, high blood pressure, liver cirrhosis and can lead to addiction.

Get enough sleep as this will help your cells renew and reinvigorate your body. Determine just how much sleep your body needs and make sure you get it. Avoid watching television, social media, web surfing, reading, or doing work in bed. Get off all devices at least an hour before your scheduled bedtime - and no mobile phone or other digital devices by your bedside!

Get up to date with your medical and dental check-ups. Deal now with any chronic aches and pains. If conventional medicine has not helped, then check out alternative and complementary therapists.

Relax and get some stillness in your life. Make relaxation a normal state of mind for you. Take up meditation or yoga. Get a massage once or twice a month. Have regular holidays that give your body and mind a chance to rest and recuperate.

Begin to take total self-care today, and you will enjoy life so much more once you have optimum health. Life becomes a joy, and you will have the energy, passion, and drive to make the most of it.

**Remember, you owe it to yourself to be the healthiest you can be. Start today, reclaim your birth right and get the healthy life you deserve.**

## Power Actions to Take Total Self-Care

Write down up to 10 things that you will undertake to do in the next seven days, as part of your regime of total self-care. *For example, arrange a dental or medical check, join a gym, enrol for yoga classes.*

1. . . . . . . . . . . . . . . . . . . . . . . . . . . . . . . . . . . . . . . . . . . . . . . . . . . .

2. . . . . . . . . . . . . . . . . . . . . . . . . . . . . . . . . . . . . . . . . . . . . . . . . . . .

3. . . . . . . . . . . . . . . . . . . . . . . . . . . . . . . . . . . . . . . . . . . . . . . . . . . .

4. . . . . . . . . . . . . . . . . . . . . . . . . . . . . . . . . . . . . . . . . . . . . . . . . . . .

5. . . . . . . . . . . . . . . . . . . . . . . . . . . . . . . . . . . . . . . . . . . . . . . . . . . .

6. . . . . . . . . . . . . . . . . . . . . . . . . . . . . . . . . . . . . . . . . . . . . . . . . . . .

7. . . . . . . . . . . . . . . . . . . . . . . . . . . . . . . . . . . . . . . . . . . . . . . . . . . .

8. . . . . . . . . . . . . . . . . . . . . . . . . . . . . . . . . . . . . . . . . . . . . . . . . . . .

9. . . . . . . . . . . . . . . . . . . . . . . . . . . . . . . . . . . . . . . . . . . . . . . . . . . .

10. . . . . . . . . . . . . . . . . . . . . . . . . . . . . . . . . . . . . . . . . . . . . . . . . . .

List five self-care habits that you will introduce into your life over the next fourteen days. *For example, these might include taking more exercise, or getting adequate sleep.*

What support, if any, do you need to make this happen?

1. . . . . . . . . . . . . . . . . . . . . . . . . . . . . . . . . . . . . . . . . . . . . . . . . . . .
   . . . . . . . . . . . . . . . . . . . . . . . . . . . . . . . . . . . . . . . . . . . . . . . . . . .

2. . . . . . . . . . . . . . . . . . . . . . . . . . . . . . . . . . . . . . . . . . . . . . . . . . . .
   . . . . . . . . . . . . . . . . . . . . . . . . . . . . . . . . . . . . . . . . . . . . . . . . . . .

3. . . . . . . . . . . . . . . . . . . . . . . . . . . . . . . . . . . . . . . . . . . . . . . . . . . .
   . . . . . . . . . . . . . . . . . . . . . . . . . . . . . . . . . . . . . . . . . . . . . . . . . . .

4. . . . . . . . . . . . . . . . . . . . . . . . . . . . . . . . . . . . . . . . . . . . . . . . . . . .
   . . . . . . . . . . . . . . . . . . . . . . . . . . . . . . . . . . . . . . . . . . . . . . . . . . .

5. . . . . . . . . . . . . . . . . . . . . . . . . . . . . . . . . . . . . . . . . . . . . . . . . . . .
   . . . . . . . . . . . . . . . . . . . . . . . . . . . . . . . . . . . . . . . . . . . . . . . . . . .

Write down up to five things you will give up – and by when. *For example, smoking, caffeine, junk food.*

What support, if any, do you need to make this happen?

1. . . . . . . . . . . . . . . . . . . . . . . . . . . . . . . . . . . . . . . . . . . . . . . . . .
   . . . . . . . . . . . . . . . . . . . . . . . . . . . . . . . . . . . . . . . . . . . . . . . . .

2. . . . . . . . . . . . . . . . . . . . . . . . . . . . . . . . . . . . . . . . . . . . . . . . . .
   . . . . . . . . . . . . . . . . . . . . . . . . . . . . . . . . . . . . . . . . . . . . . . . . .

3. . . . . . . . . . . . . . . . . . . . . . . . . . . . . . . . . . . . . . . . . . . . . . . . . .
   . . . . . . . . . . . . . . . . . . . . . . . . . . . . . . . . . . . . . . . . . . . . . . . . .

4. . . . . . . . . . . . . . . . . . . . . . . . . . . . . . . . . . . . . . . . . . . . . . . . . .
   . . . . . . . . . . . . . . . . . . . . . . . . . . . . . . . . . . . . . . . . . . . . . . . . .

5. . . . . . . . . . . . . . . . . . . . . . . . . . . . . . . . . . . . . . . . . . . . . . . . . .
   . . . . . . . . . . . . . . . . . . . . . . . . . . . . . . . . . . . . . . . . . . . . . . . . .

List five things you will begin to have more of – and by when. *Consider things such as drinking more water, having regular quiet time, going out in the fresh air.*

|  | Action | Date |
|---|---|---|
| 1. | . . . . . . . . . . . . . . . . . . . . . . . . . . . . . . . . . . . . | . . . . . . . . . . |
|  | . . . . . . . . . . . . . . . . . . . . . . . . . . . . . . . . . . . . | . . . . . . . . . . |
| 2. | . . . . . . . . . . . . . . . . . . . . . . . . . . . . . . . . . . . . | . . . . . . . . . . |
|  | . . . . . . . . . . . . . . . . . . . . . . . . . . . . . . . . . . . . | . . . . . . . . . . |
| 3. | . . . . . . . . . . . . . . . . . . . . . . . . . . . . . . . . . . . . | . . . . . . . . . . |
|  | . . . . . . . . . . . . . . . . . . . . . . . . . . . . . . . . . . . . | . . . . . . . . . . |
| 4. | . . . . . . . . . . . . . . . . . . . . . . . . . . . . . . . . . . . . | . . . . . . . . . . |
|  | . . . . . . . . . . . . . . . . . . . . . . . . . . . . . . . . . . . . | . . . . . . . . . . |
| 5. | . . . . . . . . . . . . . . . . . . . . . . . . . . . . . . . . . . . . | . . . . . . . . . . |
|  | . . . . . . . . . . . . . . . . . . . . . . . . . . . . . . . . . . . . | . . . . . . . . . . |

## 20 – INCREASE YOUR ENERGY AND ZEST FOR LIFE

To create the life you love and to live it, you will need lots of energy to live it to the full, and to do everything you would like to.

You can indeed have all the energy and support you need in your life. Simply get clear on what you need to do to make it happen.

The way you manage your natural energy will have an enormous impact on your ability to perform well and at consistently high levels. What are your healthy sources of energy? What drains you? Reflect on what new activities and habits you are willing to take on.

**Performing well and at your peak requires that you balance energy expenditure with energy renewal, and it is therefore vital that you continually replenish your energy.**

I have always had a lot of energy – to the point of people considering me hyperactive! I would like to think that I have now mellowed and have just as much energy as before, but much more channelled.

Previously, I usually managed to get everything done that I wanted each day, but quite often ended up being exhausted and worn out. Part of this was due to a habit of giving and doing things for others. I used to just give, give, and give without re-charging my batteries. By putting others before me like this, I was being totally detrimental to myself.

Then one day I got my wake-up call when my body simply gave up and I fell ill through sheer exhaustion. I had not had a proper break for months and I simply crashed out for a few days at home. I now have a much better balance and sensible self-care habits. I consider my needs and priorities first – and I mean that in a non-selfish way.

I now also ask for help and support from the people around me. I have learnt to work around my fiercely independent nature whilst also allowing others to help me for a change.

When a certain task or situation seems too daunting or draining, look to delegate wherever possible and as appropriate. Look for help from someone else who also has a commitment to this task or situation.

Giving something away that you are reluctant to deal with might just open a great opportunity for someone else to grow. And if you do have to deal with the situation yourself, just think about how much better you will feel once it is finally resolved and imagine what you can do with all the energy you will reclaim in the future as a result.

Start your day with an invigorating shower. Go even further and turn on the cold water for a few seconds. You will be thankful for the rest of the day.

Begin your working day with a list of things you must do in that day and cross them off as you achieve them. It will energise you to see the list get shorter. Prioritise your list and focus your energy on one task at a time, until it is complete.

Do not start your day by looking at your smartphone and diving straight into social media or the news! I challenge you to not even look at your phone or any other digital device till later in the morning - unless your work requires to do so.

Conversely, do not spend the last hour before you go to bed on social media.

Watch what you eat. Treat yourself to a power packed lunch of carbohydrates, protein, and vegetables every day. For a snack, consider eating a handful of nuts, or a banana which will lift your blood sugar and also contains potassium to regulate your blood pressure.

Avoid being around electro-magnetic appliances such as a TV, a computer, or a mobile phone, for too long. When working on a computer, have frequent short breaks, at least five minutes every hour.

Breathe deeply and right down to your stomach. The extra oxygen will make you feel better instantly as it reaches your cells.

Put a photo or picture of an energising scene on your wall in your office or home and reflect on the scenery whenever you feel yourself flagging. Visualise a time when you have felt really energised, such as on holiday, and fix it in your mind.

**Walk for at least 30 minutes every day, even if it is just around the block.**

If you must carry your mobile phone as you walk, then consider using it to track your steps and aim for 10,000 steps per day. Ideally find a local park or maybe even a fountain to reconnect you with the earth and the elements.

Spend some quality time by yourself every day. This could be something as simple as putting your feet up for 15 minutes. Explore ways of bringing more stillness and quiet time in your life such as through meditation, early morning walks in the park and listening to soothing music.

Have a break at weekends and regular vacations to re-energise you. Spend as much time as possible with loved ones, children, animals – reconnect with the child in you.

Get connected with what gives you energy and what drains you. Mix with inspiring grounded people.

Conversely, minimise the amount of time you spend around people who drain you. Know that it is within your control to cut loose those things in your life – relationships, situations, activities, habits, and obligations – that drain your energy. By doing so, you can then create an environment that supports and boosts your energy, thereby making room for better things to come in.

Connect with your passion – do spend time pursuing your favourite hobby or sport. Watching sport may well be your passion and you will get energised as the adrenalin gets going.

Your increased energy will free you up to maximise your creativity and put your talents to the best use. You will then be on your way to create the kind of life you desire in less time and with greater enjoyment.

Being energised can then become a natural state of being where you will feel more relaxed and able to achieve much more and with less effort.

**Being in your natural energised state every day means you are sure to have even more zest and vitality for living your life to the full.**

## Power Actions to Increase Your Energy and Zest for Life

Visualise a time when you have felt really energised. Write a few sentences on where you were and what you were doing.

. . . . . . . . . . . . . . . . . . . . . . . . . . . . . . . . . . . . . . . . . . . . . . . . . . . . .
. . . . . . . . . . . . . . . . . . . . . . . . . . . . . . . . . . . . . . . . . . . . . . . . . . . . .
. . . . . . . . . . . . . . . . . . . . . . . . . . . . . . . . . . . . . . . . . . . . . . . . . . . . .
. . . . . . . . . . . . . . . . . . . . . . . . . . . . . . . . . . . . . . . . . . . . . . . . . . . . .
. . . . . . . . . . . . . . . . . . . . . . . . . . . . . . . . . . . . . . . . . . . . . . . . . . . . .
. . . . . . . . . . . . . . . . . . . . . . . . . . . . . . . . . . . . . . . . . . . . . . . . . . . . .
. . . . . . . . . . . . . . . . . . . . . . . . . . . . . . . . . . . . . . . . . . . . . . . . . . . . .
. . . . . . . . . . . . . . . . . . . . . . . . . . . . . . . . . . . . . . . . . . . . . . . . . . . . .
. . . . . . . . . . . . . . . . . . . . . . . . . . . . . . . . . . . . . . . . . . . . . . . . . . . . .

Write down five great things about that time. What were your feelings? From now on, reconnect with these feelings any time you want to get energised even more.

1. . . . . . . . . . . . . . . . . . . . . . . . . . . . . . . . . . . . . . . . . . . . . . . . . . .
. . . . . . . . . . . . . . . . . . . . . . . . . . . . . . . . . . . . . . . . . . . . . . . . .

2. . . . . . . . . . . . . . . . . . . . . . . . . . . . . . . . . . . . . . . . . . . . . . . . . . .
. . . . . . . . . . . . . . . . . . . . . . . . . . . . . . . . . . . . . . . . . . . . . . . . .

3. . . . . . . . . . . . . . . . . . . . . . . . . . . . . . . . . . . . . . . . . . . . . . . . . . .
. . . . . . . . . . . . . . . . . . . . . . . . . . . . . . . . . . . . . . . . . . . . . . . . .

4. . . . . . . . . . . . . . . . . . . . . . . . . . . . . . . . . . . . . . . . . . . . . . . . . . .
. . . . . . . . . . . . . . . . . . . . . . . . . . . . . . . . . . . . . . . . . . . . . . . . .

5. . . . . . . . . . . . . . . . . . . . . . . . . . . . . . . . . . . . . . . . . . . . . . . . . . .
. . . . . . . . . . . . . . . . . . . . . . . . . . . . . . . . . . . . . . . . . . . . . . . . .

What situations, activities, habits, obligations, or relationships are draining your energy? Identify three of them, big or small that you wish to change or let go in the next 14 days and outline what you will do to change that.

1. . . . . . . . . . . . . . . . . . . . . . . . . . . . . . . . . . . . . . . . . . . . . . . . .

   . . . . . . . . . . . . . . . . . . . . . . . . . . . . . . . . . . . . . . . . . . . . . . . .

2. . . . . . . . . . . . . . . . . . . . . . . . . . . . . . . . . . . . . . . . . . . . . . . . .

   . . . . . . . . . . . . . . . . . . . . . . . . . . . . . . . . . . . . . . . . . . . . . . . .

3. . . . . . . . . . . . . . . . . . . . . . . . . . . . . . . . . . . . . . . . . . . . . . . . .

   . . . . . . . . . . . . . . . . . . . . . . . . . . . . . . . . . . . . . . . . . . . . . . . .


List five things you will do in the next seven days to increase your energy. *For example, eating nutritious food, spending a lot less time on your phone and on social media, improving your work area, delegating, taking walks at lunchtime, and breathing deeper.*

1. . . . . . . . . . . . . . . . . . . . . . . . . . . . . . . . . . . . . . . . . . . . . . . . .

2. . . . . . . . . . . . . . . . . . . . . . . . . . . . . . . . . . . . . . . . . . . . . . . . .

3. . . . . . . . . . . . . . . . . . . . . . . . . . . . . . . . . . . . . . . . . . . . . . . . .

4. . . . . . . . . . . . . . . . . . . . . . . . . . . . . . . . . . . . . . . . . . . . . . . . .

5. . . . . . . . . . . . . . . . . . . . . . . . . . . . . . . . . . . . . . . . . . . . . . . . .


List three things you can do to bring more stillness and quiet time into your life. *For example, meditation, walks in nature, listening to soothing music.*

1. . . . . . . . . . . . . . . . . . . . . . . . . . . . . . . . . . . . . . . . . . . . . . . . .

   . . . . . . . . . . . . . . . . . . . . . . . . . . . . . . . . . . . . . . . . . . . . . . . .

2. . . . . . . . . . . . . . . . . . . . . . . . . . . . . . . . . . . . . . . . . . . . . . . . .

   . . . . . . . . . . . . . . . . . . . . . . . . . . . . . . . . . . . . . . . . . . . . . . . .

3. . . . . . . . . . . . . . . . . . . . . . . . . . . . . . . . . . . . . . . . . . . . . . . . .

   . . . . . . . . . . . . . . . . . . . . . . . . . . . . . . . . . . . . . . . . . . . . . . . .

## 21 – IMPROVE ALL YOUR RELATIONSHIPS

**T**o create the life you love, you want to have great relationships with everyone in your life.

People will come and go, but their impact and their essence remain with you forever. It is up to you what you make of their presence in your life. Every person has a 'gift' for you – a lesson. Ask what you can learn and receive in each relationship.

Some people you meet have so much love in them you can feel it in their presence and see it in their eyes. They simply cannot do enough for you. I have been lucky enough to have such a friend who is also a homeopath whom I see regularly. She is one of the most loving persons I have ever met and her presence in my life continues to be a gift for others and me.

Through the course of my work, I meet many people, and once I was involved with a project that ultimately failed to get off the ground. I realised afterwards that there was a lot of negativity surrounding some of the people involved, and though the project was abandoned, I was blessed with some new friends, such as the friend who edited this book!

I seem to have a gift of connecting very easily and quickly with all types of people and creating great relationships, friendships, and business partnerships. I continue to meet amazing people from all the variety of events and activities I take part in. You too can do the same as you grow.

I have now worked out that I get on so well with others as I almost subconsciously look to see how I can help and support them. I am also very open and honest in my dealings. People seem to get this, and this leads to truly harmonious relationships with almost everyone in my life now.

Of course, this was not always the case and in the past I have had my fair share of fallouts. Only recently I had a major misunderstanding with a friend to the point that I deleted her contact details from my mobile phone. Then two months later, she called me out of the blue and we gave each other the grace to clear up the air between us. Our friendship has now resumed and is stronger than before due to this clarification.

**The key is to know that people really appreciate honesty and openness in relationships. Always be true to your word and tell it how it is for you. Speak your truth directly and authentically.**

This doesn't though mean you can be brutally rude. It is important to also be respectful of other people's feelings and opinions. Be tactful as appropriate to the situation.

Show your appreciation in all areas of your life. Keep a count of the number of times you say 'thank you' every day and keep increasing. Say your thanks genuinely and wholeheartedly to your partner, colleagues, family; and especially to all those strangers who do so much to make your life convenient and easy, such as shop assistants, the postman and the dustman.

**The greatest gift you can give people is your presence and undivided attention.**

When people are talking to you, stop what you are doing, look straight at them and avoid all distractions and interruptions. No looking at your phone whilst you are in a conversation!

Practise your listening skills, focus completely on that person and be present. Truly listen to them. Your undivided attention tells the other person that you genuinely value them.

Be interested in other people. The emphasis here is on being interested rather than 'interesting'. Be genuine about this and do not fake it.

Make other people feel important, show everyone that they count and raise their self-esteem. And by doing so, you will raise your own self-esteem too.

Don't take things personally. What anyone says or does to you is merely a reflection of their own reality. Become immune to what others say and do when it seems negative or hurtful. See it as a gift to you and an opportunity for you to help them.

Stop criticising yourself and others. Criticism can be so demoralising and destructive for adults and children alike. Become aware of how you speak to the people you care about and recognise when you are being critical. Ask people for genuine and open feedback about your habits of criticism and be big enough to change your ways.

Truly empathise with other people. Start to listen and understand their point of view. This will help avoid arguments and save you draining your energy. Anytime you are in a tricky situation, put yourself in their shoes and ask yourself how you would like to be treated. Remember the old saying – do unto others what you would have done to you.

Stop dumping on others. Do not relieve your own stress by taking it out on someone close to you – this does not help either of you.

**Focus on changing yourself – accept and realise that you cannot change anyone else.**

If a situation bothers you so much, then change it or change your attitude to it. It is all about you and what you bring to any relationship.

Do not make assumptions about other people and situations. Communicate clearly, to avoid misunderstandings and conflict. Ask for clarification anytime you are not clear about something. Speak up even if you feel you might sound stupid or naïve – better to be clear now than to have a falling out later. The other person will also appreciate where you are coming from.

Stop gossiping about others as it will inevitably come back to you and affect your relationships. Assume that anyone you are talking about can actually hear what you are saying about them. Learn to only say good things about others – by doing this one thing alone, your relationships will soon improve.

Assess where improvement is needed in your relationships and get committed to improving them.

**One of the blessings of a creating and living a wonderful life is loving and fulfilling relationships with everyone around you.**

## Power Actions to Improve all Your Relationships

Review your relationships and assess where improvements can be made. Can you identify any patterns?

. . . . . . . . . . . . . . . . . . . . . . . . . . . . . . . . . . . . . . . . . . . . . . . . . . . .

. . . . . . . . . . . . . . . . . . . . . . . . . . . . . . . . . . . . . . . . . . . . . . . . . . . .

. . . . . . . . . . . . . . . . . . . . . . . . . . . . . . . . . . . . . . . . . . . . . . . . . . . .

. . . . . . . . . . . . . . . . . . . . . . . . . . . . . . . . . . . . . . . . . . . . . . . . . . . .

. . . . . . . . . . . . . . . . . . . . . . . . . . . . . . . . . . . . . . . . . . . . . . . . . . . .

. . . . . . . . . . . . . . . . . . . . . . . . . . . . . . . . . . . . . . . . . . . . . . . . . . . .

. . . . . . . . . . . . . . . . . . . . . . . . . . . . . . . . . . . . . . . . . . . . . . . . . . . .

. . . . . . . . . . . . . . . . . . . . . . . . . . . . . . . . . . . . . . . . . . . . . . . . . . . .

. . . . . . . . . . . . . . . . . . . . . . . . . . . . . . . . . . . . . . . . . . . . . . . . . . . .

. . . . . . . . . . . . . . . . . . . . . . . . . . . . . . . . . . . . . . . . . . . . . . . . . . . .

List up to 10 ways you can start improving the relationships in your life.

1. . . . . . . . . . . . . . . . . . . . . . . . . . . . . . . . . . . . . . . . . . . . . . . . .

2. . . . . . . . . . . . . . . . . . . . . . . . . . . . . . . . . . . . . . . . . . . . . . . . .

3. . . . . . . . . . . . . . . . . . . . . . . . . . . . . . . . . . . . . . . . . . . . . . . . .

4. . . . . . . . . . . . . . . . . . . . . . . . . . . . . . . . . . . . . . . . . . . . . . . . .

5. . . . . . . . . . . . . . . . . . . . . . . . . . . . . . . . . . . . . . . . . . . . . . . . .

6. . . . . . . . . . . . . . . . . . . . . . . . . . . . . . . . . . . . . . . . . . . . . . . . .

7. . . . . . . . . . . . . . . . . . . . . . . . . . . . . . . . . . . . . . . . . . . . . . . . .

8. . . . . . . . . . . . . . . . . . . . . . . . . . . . . . . . . . . . . . . . . . . . . . . . .

9. . . . . . . . . . . . . . . . . . . . . . . . . . . . . . . . . . . . . . . . . . . . . . . . .

10. . . . . . . . . . . . . . . . . . . . . . . . . . . . . . . . . . . . . . . . . . . . . . . . .

Think of five people in your life, with whom you would like to improve your relationship.

1. . . . . . . . . . . . . . . . . . . . . . . . . . . . . . . . . . . . . . . . . . . . . . . . . . . . . . . . .

2. . . . . . . . . . . . . . . . . . . . . . . . . . . . . . . . . . . . . . . . . . . . . . . . . . . . . . . . .

3. . . . . . . . . . . . . . . . . . . . . . . . . . . . . . . . . . . . . . . . . . . . . . . . . . . . . . . . .

4. . . . . . . . . . . . . . . . . . . . . . . . . . . . . . . . . . . . . . . . . . . . . . . . . . . . . . . . .

5. . . . . . . . . . . . . . . . . . . . . . . . . . . . . . . . . . . . . . . . . . . . . . . . . . . . . . . . .

List five things you will do in the next seven days, to improve your relationships with these people.

1. . . . . . . . . . . . . . . . . . . . . . . . . . . . . . . . . . . . . . . . . . . . . . . . . . . . . . . . .

. . . . . . . . . . . . . . . . . . . . . . . . . . . . . . . . . . . . . . . . . . . . . . . . . . . . . . . .

2. . . . . . . . . . . . . . . . . . . . . . . . . . . . . . . . . . . . . . . . . . . . . . . . . . . . . . . . .

. . . . . . . . . . . . . . . . . . . . . . . . . . . . . . . . . . . . . . . . . . . . . . . . . . . . . . . .

3. . . . . . . . . . . . . . . . . . . . . . . . . . . . . . . . . . . . . . . . . . . . . . . . . . . . . . . . .

. . . . . . . . . . . . . . . . . . . . . . . . . . . . . . . . . . . . . . . . . . . . . . . . . . . . . . . .

4. . . . . . . . . . . . . . . . . . . . . . . . . . . . . . . . . . . . . . . . . . . . . . . . . . . . . . . . .

. . . . . . . . . . . . . . . . . . . . . . . . . . . . . . . . . . . . . . . . . . . . . . . . . . . . . . . .

5. . . . . . . . . . . . . . . . . . . . . . . . . . . . . . . . . . . . . . . . . . . . . . . . . . . . . . . . .

. . . . . . . . . . . . . . . . . . . . . . . . . . . . . . . . . . . . . . . . . . . . . . . . . . . . . . . .

Write down what you did and how the relationship has improved.

. . . . . . . . . . . . . . . . . . . . . . . . . . . . . . . . . . . . . . . . . . . . . . . . . . . . . . . . . .

. . . . . . . . . . . . . . . . . . . . . . . . . . . . . . . . . . . . . . . . . . . . . . . . . . . . . . . . . .

. . . . . . . . . . . . . . . . . . . . . . . . . . . . . . . . . . . . . . . . . . . . . . . . . . . . . . . . . .

. . . . . . . . . . . . . . . . . . . . . . . . . . . . . . . . . . . . . . . . . . . . . . . . . . . . . . . . . .

. . . . . . . . . . . . . . . . . . . . . . . . . . . . . . . . . . . . . . . . . . . . . . . . . . . . . . . . . .

## 22 - ENJOY YOUR SINGLE LIFE

**I** f you are single and wish to enjoy life as a single person, then this chapter is for you. If not, then please move on to chapter 23.

As you create and live the life you love, you can choose to live your life either as a single person or you could be in a relationship.

Many single people wait until they are in a relationship before beginning to live their life. But you can be happy right now, either single or with a partner.

**Your life is happening today, and it is not a dress rehearsal for the day you are in a relationship.**

Being single gives you a lot of flexibility and independence. I remember having had some great moments in my life when I have been single. Having a fierce streak of independence means that I can go off and do what I wish and when I want to.

It is also important for me to meet like-minded people and I believe that being single has helped me achieve this in the past. On reflection, maybe this would have happened even if I had been in a relationship at the time, but I just loved the freedom I had being single.

If you choose to be single or if you are in between relationships, rather than getting hung up over not being with someone, focus on what you have right now and on creating a terrific single life.

Ask yourself what your life is going to be about. What do you enjoy doing?

Reflect on what you want to contribute to the world, where you want to live and how much money you want to make. The key is to make yourself truly happy right now and to remain happy, regardless of whether you are single or with a partner.

Some single people throw themselves into their business or career and forgo pleasure time and self-care. It is as if their accomplishments are the only things that matter.

Pamper and treat yourself every day with something luxurious and pleasurable. This can be as simple as a 10-minute walk, a drink at the local coffee shop, a body lotion that smells good, or even a candle-lit bath and so on. Do whatever does it for you. Such treats are not just reserved for a partner to give you as gifts.

**Create a life full of such delicious moments and your whole outlook will soon improve.**

Be passionate about your life. Have a vision for your life and live by it every day. Have a purpose for getting out of bed every morning. What activity energises you? What makes time stop for you?

Your life purpose is your own, whether you are single or with a partner, and you will be happiest when fully living your life purpose. Having a partner is not a substitute for a meaningful life.

Build a community of friends and like-minded people. Socialise, have fun, and join clubs around your favourite topics. Reach out to people already in your life and strengthen your communal ties. You will be creating a varied rich life. You will also then have people in your life who care about you and your life, and who are meeting many of your needs. This will make you less needy and more attractive to a potential partner if that is what you ultimately desire.

At the time of writing, I am single and loving every moment of it. I have created a wonderful community of people in my life – friends, business associates and clients – and more amazing people continue to show up in my life.

I feel very nurtured, supported and am very grateful to all these people being in my life. It is like having a whole orchestra of people rooting for my success and well-being.

Start doing the things that you have been putting off doing till you had a partner. Find one fun thing to do every week and cross it off your list. One day you can do them all again with your partner if you wish.

Put the past in the past where it belongs. Be complete with past relationships and let go of any baggage. Stop hanging on to unhappy moments from the past. Let go of hurts and resentments towards anyone. It takes courage and application to do this, but you will benefit greatly in the long run.

Improve your relationship skills. Read all you can around this topic, both online and in books, magazines, and newspapers. Check out relationship workshops and seminars. Go and have some fun at dating: you could find local dating events, singles dinners, theatre events, or even try speed dating.

Just because you may have been single for a while does not mean that you won't have a successful lifelong relationship if that is what you desire – learn and apply new skills.

Appreciate and value what goodness you already have in your life right now. Being single gives you true freedom and independence to do exactly what you choose with your time and resources – and you can choose who to do it with. The world is truly your oyster.

**Remember: as you create a life you love, you can choose to live it and be happy, either as a single person or with a partner.**

## Power Actions to Enjoy Your Single Life

List 10 great things about your life as a single person.

1. ........................................................

2. ........................................................

3. ........................................................

4. ........................................................

5. ........................................................

6. ........................................................

7. ........................................................

8. ........................................................

9. ........................................................

10. ........................................................

List five things you will do to pamper yourself in the next seven days.

1. ........................................................
   ........................................................

2. ........................................................
   ........................................................

3. ........................................................
   ........................................................

4. ........................................................
   ........................................................

5. ........................................................
   ........................................................

If you are single, write down five activities that you have been putting off until you are in a relationship. Put a date against each for when you will have done these activities.

Action                                                                      Date

1. . . . . . . . . . . . . . . . . . . . . . . . . . . . . . . . . . . . . . . . . . .        . . . . . . . . . .

. . . . . . . . . . . . . . . . . . . . . . . . . . . . . . . . . . . . . . . . . .        . . . . . . . . . .

2. . . . . . . . . . . . . . . . . . . . . . . . . . . . . . . . . . . . . . . . . . .        . . . . . . . . . .

. . . . . . . . . . . . . . . . . . . . . . . . . . . . . . . . . . . . . . . . . .        . . . . . . . . . .

3. . . . . . . . . . . . . . . . . . . . . . . . . . . . . . . . . . . . . . . . . . .        . . . . . . . . . .

. . . . . . . . . . . . . . . . . . . . . . . . . . . . . . . . . . . . . . . . . .        . . . . . . . . . .

4. . . . . . . . . . . . . . . . . . . . . . . . . . . . . . . . . . . . . . . . . . .        . . . . . . . . . .

. . . . . . . . . . . . . . . . . . . . . . . . . . . . . . . . . . . . . . . . . .        . . . . . . . . . .

5. . . . . . . . . . . . . . . . . . . . . . . . . . . . . . . . . . . . . . . . . . .        . . . . . . . . . .

. . . . . . . . . . . . . . . . . . . . . . . . . . . . . . . . . . . . . . . . . .        . . . . . . . . . .

List three areas of interest that you want to develop further. Put a date against each indicating when you will start these.

Area of interest                                                            Date

1. . . . . . . . . . . . . . . . . . . . . . . . . . . . . . . . . . . . . . . . . . .        . . . . . . . . . .

. . . . . . . . . . . . . . . . . . . . . . . . . . . . . . . . . . . . . . . . . .        . . . . . . . . . .

2. . . . . . . . . . . . . . . . . . . . . . . . . . . . . . . . . . . . . . . . . . .        . . . . . . . . . .

. . . . . . . . . . . . . . . . . . . . . . . . . . . . . . . . . . . . . . . . . .        . . . . . . . . . .

3. . . . . . . . . . . . . . . . . . . . . . . . . . . . . . . . . . . . . . . . . . .        . . . . . . . . . .

. . . . . . . . . . . . . . . . . . . . . . . . . . . . . . . . . . . . . . . . . .        . . . . . . . . . .

## 23 - CREATE YOUR DREAM RELATIONSHIP

**A**s you get the life you love, you might want to also create a dream relationship. Everyone dreams of that ideal relationship – one that is full of love and affection. A relationship with someone that you connect with mentally, physically, emotionally, and spiritually. We all want to meet our 'soul mate'.

To create such a relationship, focus on creating the kind of life you truly want, rather than on attracting a partner and wanting a relationship. Be happy, regardless of whether you are in a relationship or not. The key thing is to focus on creating your ideal life. The kind of life that excites you so much that you jump out of bed every morning. Once you are in such a place, your dream partner can simply walk in and join you.

In the past when I have been in relationships, and they have not worked out it has been mainly because of work that I needed to do on myself and areas in my life that I still had to improve. Looking back, I had become focussed on getting into a relationship for the sake of it rather than looking at ways of improving my life overall.

**A dream relationship should be the icing on the cake that is your life and getting into a relationship should not be the main and only focus of your life.**

Get clear on what your ideal life is going to be about. What do you enjoy doing? What do you do for a living? Reflect on what you want to contribute to the world, where you want to live and how much money you want to make. The key is to make yourself truly happy right now and to also remain happy regardless of whether you are in a relationship or not.

Get clear about what you want in a relationship. Make the fulfilment of your short term and long term needs the criteria for choosing a partner.

Define and get clear about your ideal relationship and partner. Be realistic. Ask what your needs are, rather than your wants. What qualities must your relationship have? What are the absolute essentials for you to thrive? Which criteria are simply not negotiable? You deserve the best you can get – and do not compromise.

As I write this, I am currently single and have chosen to be so for the time being. I have gained a lot of clarity about what I desire in my ideal partner and in my ideal relationship. It is wonderful to have such clarity as I am no longer attracting anyone who does not meet my criteria.

Be complete with past relationships. Drop the baggage from the past. Let go of any hurts and resentments. Forgive that ex-partner who was mean to you. The true test of your growth is to meet such a person from your past and to not feel any negative thoughts.

A couple of years after we separated, my ex-wife and I had a wonderful exchange of emails full of love, reconciliation, and forgiveness. Thanks to the wonders of modern technology, for me that was the defining moment when I felt complete with her. We were able to let each other happily move forward with our lives.

Ironically, I am probably now the sort of person she always wanted me to be, but she had to let me go for me to become that.

Take stock of how you have behaved in previous relationships. If your past relationships have not worked out for whatever reason, then like it or not, that makes you at least 50% responsible for them not working out. Get clarity on what you contributed to those relationships not working out. Be kind to yourself as you do this. Do not make it an excuse to beat yourself up all over again.

Looking back on my relationships, I was sometimes quite selfish, and wasn't always considerate to my ex-partners, but having this awareness and hindsight does not make me think of myself in a lesser light. I was doing the best I could with the knowledge, awareness and understanding I had at the time. I look back with gratitude to my ex-partners, as they contributed to my growth and allowed me to become a better person.

Review your beliefs about relationships and look at how they may have hindered you. What do you think should happen at different stages – from courtship to living together? Reflect on what your entrenched beliefs are about the opposite sex. For example, consider if you have any fixed views on what the expected roles and duties of a partner are.

**Socialise and have fun to create a varied, rich life, to be part of a healthy supportive community and to enhance your life.**

You will therefore focus not so much on meeting someone suitable but more on creating a rich vibrant life, one which will be more attractive to a potential new partner. Most people usually socialise in various ways to meet their dream partner. But by simply just having more fun and enjoying your life, you will become so much more attractive.

Do go to things like speed dating events where you can meet more varied people. Just treat these as fun and social events. The trick with making the most of these events is to focus on your best points and be proud of that. For example, you may have a great - so show it off.

There are now so many dating apps on your phone to help you connect with and meet potential partners. Do your research and choose the app that meets your requirements and budget.

As you create your dating profile, do be honest and upfront about what you are looking for and why. Showcase your recent images which show you in your true essence and use the apps as an opportunity to meet varied and many potential partners.

Be light-hearted and have some fun with your dating – continue to give out positive energy as you meet potential partners and do not get attached to the outcome.

Make your life work for you, and then make room for your ideal partner. Once your life is working and you are happy, you will attract the right partner into your life.

You deserve the best and that includes a dream relationship and the dream partner. Do not accept second best and settle for a relationship that is not right for you.

**As you create the life you love, become clear about what you want in your life partner and why – and you will be on your way to creating that ideal relationship.**

# Power Actions to Create Your Dream Relationship

Write down up to 10 qualities that your ideal partner must have.

1. . . . . . . . . . . . . . . . . . . . . . . . . . . . . . . . . . . . . . . . . . . . . . . .

2. . . . . . . . . . . . . . . . . . . . . . . . . . . . . . . . . . . . . . . . . . . . . . . .

3. . . . . . . . . . . . . . . . . . . . . . . . . . . . . . . . . . . . . . . . . . . . . . . .

4. . . . . . . . . . . . . . . . . . . . . . . . . . . . . . . . . . . . . . . . . . . . . . . .

5. . . . . . . . . . . . . . . . . . . . . . . . . . . . . . . . . . . . . . . . . . . . . . . .

6. . . . . . . . . . . . . . . . . . . . . . . . . . . . . . . . . . . . . . . . . . . . . . . .

7. . . . . . . . . . . . . . . . . . . . . . . . . . . . . . . . . . . . . . . . . . . . . . . .

8. . . . . . . . . . . . . . . . . . . . . . . . . . . . . . . . . . . . . . . . . . . . . . . .

9. . . . . . . . . . . . . . . . . . . . . . . . . . . . . . . . . . . . . . . . . . . . . . . .

10. . . . . . . . . . . . . . . . . . . . . . . . . . . . . . . . . . . . . . . . . . . . . . . .

Note five things that you must have in your relationship.

1. . . . . . . . . . . . . . . . . . . . . . . . . . . . . . . . . . . . . . . . . . . . . . . .

2. . . . . . . . . . . . . . . . . . . . . . . . . . . . . . . . . . . . . . . . . . . . . . . .

3. . . . . . . . . . . . . . . . . . . . . . . . . . . . . . . . . . . . . . . . . . . . . . . .

4. . . . . . . . . . . . . . . . . . . . . . . . . . . . . . . . . . . . . . . . . . . . . . . .

5. . . . . . . . . . . . . . . . . . . . . . . . . . . . . . . . . . . . . . . . . . . . . . . .

Write down up to five criteria that are simply NOT acceptable in your relationship. *For example – my partner must be a non-smoker or must want children.*

1. . . . . . . . . . . . . . . . . . . . . . . . . . . . . . . . . . . . . . . . . . . . . . . .

2. . . . . . . . . . . . . . . . . . . . . . . . . . . . . . . . . . . . . . . . . . . . . . . .

3. . . . . . . . . . . . . . . . . . . . . . . . . . . . . . . . . . . . . . . . . . . . . . . .

4. . . . . . . . . . . . . . . . . . . . . . . . . . . . . . . . . . . . . . . . . . . . . . . .

5. . . . . . . . . . . . . . . . . . . . . . . . . . . . . . . . . . . . . . . . . . . . . . . .

List at least 10 great qualities about you that makes you irresistible.

1. .....................................................................

2. .....................................................................

3. .....................................................................

4. .....................................................................

5. .....................................................................

6. .....................................................................

7. .....................................................................

8. .....................................................................

9. .....................................................................

10. ....................................................................

Write down up to five things that you will do in the coming 14 days, to have fun and meet new people.

1. .....................................................................

.....................................................................

2. .....................................................................

.....................................................................

3. .....................................................................

.....................................................................

4. .....................................................................

.....................................................................

5. .....................................................................

.....................................................................

## 24 - TRANSFORM YOUR EXISTING LOVE RELATIONSHIP

**A**s you create the life you love, and you are living it, you can take your relationship with your partner to new levels.

If you are in a relationship, is it what you always dreamed about?

In a dream relationship, you bring out the best in one another and make yourself stronger together as a team than you would be apart. Such a relationship helps you become a better person and provides you with the support and nurturing that you deserve.

When I was married a few years ago, I hardly ever thought of myself as being part of a couple – in my head I planned and did things on my own and in my own way! I still cringe when I look back and realise the pain I must have caused my ex-wife.

If you have been together for a long time, you could take each other for granted. This does not imply that your love for each other is fading, simply a lack of effort. Be willing to make the time and effort for each other.

Be realistic too and accept that no one person is ever going to fulfil your every need and desire. Finding such a person and respecting your judgment in choosing that person are a prerequisite to creating a long-lasting, happy relationship.

**Truly committing yourself to someone requires self-awareness, wisdom, trust, and being open to vulnerability.**

Be clear about what you want from your love relationship. Make fulfilment of your short-term and long-term needs the criteria for choosing a partner and being in a relationship. Prepare yourself to negotiate and be open to their needs and wants too. Create, share, and renew your vision of your dream life together.

Accept your partner just as they are. Your partner is a very special human being: the only one in the world like them, with their own wonderful traits and unique gifts. Truly love and accept the whole beautiful package they came in.

They are entitled to their own decisions, hobbies, goals and hopes. Find out their deepest desires and get as excited about them as you are about yours. And remember too that this wonderful human being is prepared to spend their life with you despite knowing all your shortcomings!

Be generous and loving in all your dealings with your partner. Give unconditionally, without seeking anything back in return. Commit 100% to your partner, with zero expectation. A lot of relationships work on a 50/50 basis whereby partners do things for each other only on a tit for tat basis. And then when they feel things are not going their way, they stop giving themselves, thereby starting a downward spiral.

Instead, commit 100% to your partner, with no holding back. If your partner also gives you their commitment on the same 100% basis, then you will both have found relationship Nirvana!

Always be in integrity. Commit to tell your partner the total truth, as honesty is one of the key things people want in a relationship. Knowing they can trust you builds a zone of safety and comfort around you both.

Resolve any differences as soon as they happen. Accept responsibility for your part of the issue at stake, and do not blame your partner. The sooner you stop blaming and start talking to each other, the better you will feel.

**Never go to sleep with an unresolved issue. Last thing at night, before falling asleep, thank your partner and tell them what you love about them being in your life.**

Do not criticise. It is ok to bring up something that is bothering you, but it is simply not ok to criticise. Your partner is doing the best they can. Support them instead in becoming an even better person – you will benefit too in the long term. Never ever put them down in front of others.

I remember a horrible moment in my married life when I criticised my ex-wife's way of cooking an aubergine dish in front of her family. You could have cut the atmosphere with a knife! I immediately realised my rudeness and though I felt awful afterwards the damage had already been done.

Though we didn't really discuss this incident later that evening, it was one key episode in our married life which came up for analysis when we had marital counselling at the time we were trying to save our marriage. I remember not even apologising at the time and I was not then big enough to admit my own shortcomings – but I would like to think I am a much different and better person now.

Create a haven for your partner. Make them feel so safe and secure with you, that they drop all their defensiveness. You can help them overcome their fears with lots of tender loving care.

Show thoughtfulness and be considerate of your partner's feelings. Treat them with the utmost care and kindness.

Let go of the past. All relationships have their difficulties. Remember only the lessons learnt and forget the details. Weather the stormy moments and savour the memory of sunny days.

Always remember what brought the two of you together in the first place. What attracted you to each other? What do you admire about your partner's personality?

Have a fun date with your partner regularly and often. Spend at least one night a week simply being with each other – remember that nothing else is as important as your time together. Strengthen your relationship by putting each other first.

In an ideal relationship, you and your partner can be yourselves. You are honest and patient with each other, you accept one another, and you are kind and thoughtful. In such an open, vulnerable, and deeply caring relationship, your love is sure to grow. And as you evolve together, you are bound to keep your relationship happy, healthy, and deeply loving.

**Give your relationship the same commitment you made when you first started dating. Simply put each other first and together create the life you love – a love-filled life of joy and purpose.**

## Power Actions to Transform your Existing Love Relationship

List 10 great things that you love about your partner.

1. . . . . . . . . . . . . . . . . . . . . . . . . . . . . . . . . . . . . . . . . . . . . . . . . . . .

2. . . . . . . . . . . . . . . . . . . . . . . . . . . . . . . . . . . . . . . . . . . . . . . . . . . .

3. . . . . . . . . . . . . . . . . . . . . . . . . . . . . . . . . . . . . . . . . . . . . . . . . . . .

4. . . . . . . . . . . . . . . . . . . . . . . . . . . . . . . . . . . . . . . . . . . . . . . . . . . .

5. . . . . . . . . . . . . . . . . . . . . . . . . . . . . . . . . . . . . . . . . . . . . . . . . . . .

6. . . . . . . . . . . . . . . . . . . . . . . . . . . . . . . . . . . . . . . . . . . . . . . . . . . .

7. . . . . . . . . . . . . . . . . . . . . . . . . . . . . . . . . . . . . . . . . . . . . . . . . . . .

8. . . . . . . . . . . . . . . . . . . . . . . . . . . . . . . . . . . . . . . . . . . . . . . . . . . .

9. . . . . . . . . . . . . . . . . . . . . . . . . . . . . . . . . . . . . . . . . . . . . . . . . . . .

10. . . . . . . . . . . . . . . . . . . . . . . . . . . . . . . . . . . . . . . . . . . . . . . . . . .

Tell them one great thing that you like about them each day for the next 10 days. Make a note here what you told them. Then start all over again.

1. . . . . . . . . . . . . . . . . . . . . . . . . . . . . . . . . . . . . . . . . . . . . . . . . . . .

2. . . . . . . . . . . . . . . . . . . . . . . . . . . . . . . . . . . . . . . . . . . . . . . . . . . .

3. . . . . . . . . . . . . . . . . . . . . . . . . . . . . . . . . . . . . . . . . . . . . . . . . . . .

4. . . . . . . . . . . . . . . . . . . . . . . . . . . . . . . . . . . . . . . . . . . . . . . . . . . .

5. . . . . . . . . . . . . . . . . . . . . . . . . . . . . . . . . . . . . . . . . . . . . . . . . . . .

6. . . . . . . . . . . . . . . . . . . . . . . . . . . . . . . . . . . . . . . . . . . . . . . . . . . .

7. . . . . . . . . . . . . . . . . . . . . . . . . . . . . . . . . . . . . . . . . . . . . . . . . . . .

8. . . . . . . . . . . . . . . . . . . . . . . . . . . . . . . . . . . . . . . . . . . . . . . . . . . .

9. . . . . . . . . . . . . . . . . . . . . . . . . . . . . . . . . . . . . . . . . . . . . . . . . . . .

10. . . . . . . . . . . . . . . . . . . . . . . . . . . . . . . . . . . . . . . . . . . . . . . . . . .

Think of 10 little loving things you can do for your partner. Do at least one of these things for your partner each day over the next 10 days.

1. . . . . . . . . . . . . . . . . . . . . . . . . . . . . . . . . . . . . . . . . . . . . . . . . . . . .

2. . . . . . . . . . . . . . . . . . . . . . . . . . . . . . . . . . . . . . . . . . . . . . . . . . . . .

3. . . . . . . . . . . . . . . . . . . . . . . . . . . . . . . . . . . . . . . . . . . . . . . . . . . . .

4. . . . . . . . . . . . . . . . . . . . . . . . . . . . . . . . . . . . . . . . . . . . . . . . . . . . .

5. . . . . . . . . . . . . . . . . . . . . . . . . . . . . . . . . . . . . . . . . . . . . . . . . . . . .

6. . . . . . . . . . . . . . . . . . . . . . . . . . . . . . . . . . . . . . . . . . . . . . . . . . . . .

7. . . . . . . . . . . . . . . . . . . . . . . . . . . . . . . . . . . . . . . . . . . . . . . . . . . . .

8. . . . . . . . . . . . . . . . . . . . . . . . . . . . . . . . . . . . . . . . . . . . . . . . . . . . .

9. . . . . . . . . . . . . . . . . . . . . . . . . . . . . . . . . . . . . . . . . . . . . . . . . . . . .

10. . . . . . . . . . . . . . . . . . . . . . . . . . . . . . . . . . . . . . . . . . . . . . . . . . . .

Plan a surprise date for your partner over the next seven days. List up to five special things you will do for them during this date. Then start all over again.

1. . . . . . . . . . . . . . . . . . . . . . . . . . . . . . . . . . . . . . . . . . . . . . . . . . . . .

. . . . . . . . . . . . . . . . . . . . . . . . . . . . . . . . . . . . . . . . . . . . . . . . . . . .

2. . . . . . . . . . . . . . . . . . . . . . . . . . . . . . . . . . . . . . . . . . . . . . . . . . . . .

. . . . . . . . . . . . . . . . . . . . . . . . . . . . . . . . . . . . . . . . . . . . . . . . . . . .

3. . . . . . . . . . . . . . . . . . . . . . . . . . . . . . . . . . . . . . . . . . . . . . . . . . . . .

. . . . . . . . . . . . . . . . . . . . . . . . . . . . . . . . . . . . . . . . . . . . . . . . . . . .

4. . . . . . . . . . . . . . . . . . . . . . . . . . . . . . . . . . . . . . . . . . . . . . . . . . . . .

. . . . . . . . . . . . . . . . . . . . . . . . . . . . . . . . . . . . . . . . . . . . . . . . . . . .

5. . . . . . . . . . . . . . . . . . . . . . . . . . . . . . . . . . . . . . . . . . . . . . . . . . . . .

. . . . . . . . . . . . . . . . . . . . . . . . . . . . . . . . . . . . . . . . . . . . . . . . . . . .

## 25 – CREATE SUNSHINE ALL YEAR-ROUND IN YOUR LIFE

Once you have created the life you love, enjoy, and deserve, you can have sunshine all year round. **All you have to do is to sustain this sunshine.**

Of course, life has its ups and downs. It is your approach and attitude to your life that can make all the difference to whether you see sunshine or clouds.

Some people always seem to be happy, smiling, and full of sunshine. Others seem to believe that they have a right to be happy, and that other people should make them happy. Some people even believe that when they are not happy, they have a right to complain about it and that complaining will cause them to be happy.

In the past, I have been described as a very happy person, and most of my life I guess I have been. Like a lot of people, I have had my knocks, and my ups and downs, but I feel that I am a better person now thanks to them. Looking back at how dire my life was only a few years ago, I have done very well to have the life I now live. The key for me has been to retain a positive sunny outlook through the dark times.

Here in the UK, the weather is a major talking point, and it amazes me how many people seem to allow their mood to be dictated by the weather. It always amuses me when I hear a weather reporter describe the weather forecast as being dismal, gloomy, or miserable. Listen closely to the language used next time you are checking out the weather and depending upon where you are in the world, be prepared to be surprised.

The weather is just weather regardless of sunshine or rain and our weather reporters are affecting a whole nation's psyche with their direct implied association of our moods with the elements. The point is you can choose to feel sunny inside you, no matter what is going on outside you.

From today, determine that you will be the one who will decide your mood, come what may in your day and regardless of what else is happening in your life.

**Accept that it is okay and normal to be happy. You are not being unduly selfish, materialistic, or self-centred.**

Live your life with optimism. Think only of all the good and positive things in your life. This will generate feelings of warmth, affection, appreciation, hope, and security. It will draw even more positive things to you.

. Limit your input of negativity and avoid too much exposure to less than positive reports on social media, television, or newspapers. Stay well informed but watching news reports repeatedly about things you can do nothing about will bring dark clouds into your life.

If you are genuinely moved by a news story such as when there is a natural disaster or famine, then take some action by contributing time or money to make some impact.

Show gratitude. Just take a second and appreciate that you are alive! The very fact you are reading the words on this page is a miracle. Be happy with what you've got – do not dwell on what you still want. Focus on what is right in your life rather than what is wrong and appreciate what you have. For example, stop obsessing about wanting a slimmer body, and be grateful that you can walk.

Smile at everyone you see. Sounds simple and it is. Do this today when you go out – smile at everyone you see. You will be surprised at what comes back to you. You will feel happier, and you will be spreading happiness around you.

When feeling emotional, let it all out. Laugh, cry, scream or do anything else that you get the urge to do – whatever it takes to let out the emotions you are feeling. If you have feelings of anger, punch a cushion or pillow. or do some demanding physical exercise to get rid of any negative energy. You will feel so much better and lighter afterwards. After all, we all need to vent at times.

Make at least one friendly phone call each day, with no intention to get some business or anything else. Just a friendly hello without any expectation.

**Appreciate the natural world that is all around you. Literally stop and smell the roses. Every now and then, look at the sunset, cloud formation or trees – bask in the awesome beauty of nature.**

Eat healthy and good quality food. For a sunny outlook, determine what foods really work for you, and develop a personal way of eating that will support you. Consult a nutritionist if necessary.

Exercise regularly and make it fun. Take some time out of your day to work your muscles and strengthen your mind, body, and spirit. Remind yourself of the benefits of exercising and adopt exercise habits as part of your daily routine of self-care. Stop thinking of exercise as an option – start today. Experiment until you find something you truly enjoy.

Get adequate sleep, which will keep you shining. Determine just how much sleep your body needs and make sure you get it. Make your bedroom a peaceful place and avoid web surfing, social media, watching TV, reading, and doing work in bed. No mobile phone or other devices by your bedside!

When you are not feeling so sunny, simply remember the happy times. And you will soon begin to feel better.

Do something for someone else. Random acts of kindness are magical and giving of yourself is one of the best highs you can get. For example, let other drivers into your traffic lane. Have a friendly conversation with the cashier at the supermarket.

Become conscious of your positive acts. When you give the gift of a smile or a kind word, you create a wonderful ripple effect of sunshine that touches many and helps build bridges between everyone.

**Here's to many more weeks, months, and years of sunshine, living the life you love.**

## Power Actions to Create Sunshine All Year-Round in Your Life

Write down up to 10 things you can do to help you maintain the life you love. Resolve to do these things for the rest of your life.

1. ............................................................
2. ............................................................
3. ............................................................
4. ............................................................
5. ............................................................
6. ............................................................
7. ............................................................
8. ............................................................
9. ............................................................
10. ............................................................

List up to 10 things you will do in the next fourteen days, to bring more sunshine and happiness into your life and that of others.

1. ............................................................
2. ............................................................
3. ............................................................
4. ............................................................
5. ............................................................
6. ............................................................
7. ............................................................
8. ............................................................
9. ............................................................
10. ............................................................

For the next seven days, smile at everyone you see. Quietly send them warm wishes of love and wellbeing. Write down here what happened as a result.

. . . . . . . . . . . . . . . . . . . . . . . . . . . . . . . . . . . . . . . . . . . . . . . . . . .

. . . . . . . . . . . . . . . . . . . . . . . . . . . . . . . . . . . . . . . . . . . . . . . . . . .

. . . . . . . . . . . . . . . . . . . . . . . . . . . . . . . . . . . . . . . . . . . . . . . . . . .

. . . . . . . . . . . . . . . . . . . . . . . . . . . . . . . . . . . . . . . . . . . . . . . . . . .

. . . . . . . . . . . . . . . . . . . . . . . . . . . . . . . . . . . . . . . . . . . . . . . . . . .

. . . . . . . . . . . . . . . . . . . . . . . . . . . . . . . . . . . . . . . . . . . . . . . . . . .

. . . . . . . . . . . . . . . . . . . . . . . . . . . . . . . . . . . . . . . . . . . . . . . . . . .

Become a ray of sunshine, love, and warmth for everyone you meet from now onwards. Write down here your thoughts about being loving and kind for the rest of your life.

. . . . . . . . . . . . . . . . . . . . . . . . . . . . . . . . . . . . . . . . . . . . . . . . . . .

. . . . . . . . . . . . . . . . . . . . . . . . . . . . . . . . . . . . . . . . . . . . . . . . . . .

. . . . . . . . . . . . . . . . . . . . . . . . . . . . . . . . . . . . . . . . . . . . . . . . . . .

. . . . . . . . . . . . . . . . . . . . . . . . . . . . . . . . . . . . . . . . . . . . . . . . . . .

. . . . . . . . . . . . . . . . . . . . . . . . . . . . . . . . . . . . . . . . . . . . . . . . . . .

. . . . . . . . . . . . . . . . . . . . . . . . . . . . . . . . . . . . . . . . . . . . . . . . . . .

. . . . . . . . . . . . . . . . . . . . . . . . . . . . . . . . . . . . . . . . . . . . . . . . . . .

. . . . . . . . . . . . . . . . . . . . . . . . . . . . . . . . . . . . . . . . . . . . . . . . . . .

. . . . . . . . . . . . . . . . . . . . . . . . . . . . . . . . . . . . . . . . . . . . . . . . . . .

. . . . . . . . . . . . . . . . . . . . . . . . . . . . . . . . . . . . . . . . . . . . . . . . . . .

. . . . . . . . . . . . . . . . . . . . . . . . . . . . . . . . . . . . . . . . . . . . . . . . . . .

# FINAL WORDS FROM ARVIND – MAKE YOUR LIFE COUNT

**N**ow that you have worked through the 25 chapters in my book, you should be well on your way to creating and living the life you love. If you have done so, then I will have achieved my purpose in writing this book, as my mission is to be of service and make a difference in the world by improving the lives of everyone with whom I come into contact.

I believe in the power of contribution, connection and celebration and my vision is to build a better world bit by bit, and to serve others in building their own lives too, step by step.

My vision for the world is that one day generations of children to come will ask their parents if something called 'war' ever existed. They will wonder if people really did annihilate each other in cold blood, and how humans ever let that happen in the first place. They will also ask if children really died due to a lack of food.

I believe that it is such a vision that we must all ultimately strive for as today we have a world challenged by a rapidly growing population, increasing warfare, climate crisis and mounting environmental problems.

You may call me naive, but to live with such hope is for me the only way forward, since **'an eye for an eye makes the whole world blind'**. It was Gandhi who said this - and his wisdom, courage and inspiration are needed more than ever in the world today.

As a child, I remember listening to a speech by a famous politician on my father's giant transistor radio. He declared that world poverty would be history in another decade and that no child would ever go to sleep on an empty stomach. Those words excited me then, making me feel all tingly and lit up, and continue to inspire me now.

We lived in Kenya at the time, and the thought of all African children no longer starving was very empowering. Even then I was aware of the vast disparity in wealth and well-being between the African people, the Asians, and the Europeans, the latter two owning most of the businesses.

Yet decades since I heard that speech, world poverty is more endemic than ever and according to the UN, around 10,000 children die every day from hunger and related causes.

In my work, I engage with a lot of children from all types of cultural and social backgrounds. I often wonder just what sort of legacy we are building for them.

Children's apparent innocence about the world out there can be both heart-breaking and endearing. Yet it is this very innocence that gives me hope and inspires me that we can indeed build a better world for them. It is our responsibility, and we owe it to future generations. We can choose how we will live our lives from here onwards. We can indeed make this a better world for all of us and the generations to come if we truly put our minds and hearts into it.

So as you move forward with your life, I invite each of you to aspire to truly create and live the life you love, and also a life that will make a huge difference to others. Commit to making the world a better place in whatever way feels right for you – big or small. And then of course do it.

As Gandhi also said, be the change that you want the world to be.

**Bring peace and love into the world in every way you can but first begin with yourself.**

I remember in 2005, around the time of the Live8 concerts, there were posters all around London of Nelson Mandela promoting his 'Make Poverty History' campaign. The slogan on these posters implored a generation to claim its greatness.

**The time has come for us to claim our greatness.**

And then one day, a generation of children to come will indeed ask their parents if war and starvation ever even existed.

Please know that by working through my book, and by creating the life you love and ultimately living it, you will have helped me greatly in fulfilling my vision of the world.

Thank you.

To end, here are my final thoughts.

**Remember that your life counts – and make it count. You are unique. There is no one else like you on this planet. There never has been and never will be.**

**Do not sell yourself short. Do not sell the world short. This is your life – love it, live it. One life, one chance – grab it.**

**Get the life you love – and live it.**

# WORDS OF INSPIRATION 1

*I wrote these words in October 2003*

## Love is All That Matters

If I had a magic wand...
I would change the world in an instant.
I would provide food for all the starving people and share their joy.
I would stop wars and bring about peace.
I would show men that their enemies have the same desires, needs, and wants as they do.
I would bring out the love that is in everyone's heart.
I would get people to share and bask in the abundance all around us.
I would encourage people to slow down and appreciate the beauty around us and in us.
I would enable people to take better care of Mother Earth.
After all, everyone is doing the best they can.
But until I find my magic wand,
I will live every day of the rest of my life in such a way.
That I may never need such a magic wand.
I will use the gift of this body to create a better world through my thoughts, words, and actions.
My mouth I will use, only to spread words of encouragement, gratitude, appreciation... and never a negative word about another.
My eyes I will use, only to see the beauty in others... even where it is deeply buried, I shall seek it out.
My ears I will use, only to hear good about others.
My hands I will use, only to enhance the world and to make a lasting contribution.
Each morning I will awaken slowly, and bask in the glory of the world that is around us,
And marvel at the sheer miracle of this life.
Every day I shall strive to live my truth,
And each day I shall spread the love that is in my heart.
After all, love is all that matters.

**Arvind Devalia**

# WORDS OF INSPIRATION 2

*I have heard these words said aloud on many occasions and I get goosebumps all over me every time. These words originally written by Marianne Williamson make us all realise just how powerful and amazing we all are.*

## Our Light

Our deepest fear is not that we are inadequate.
Our deepest fear is that we are powerful beyond measure.
It is our light, not our darkness that frightens us.
We ask ourselves
Who am I to be so brilliant, gorgeous, talented, fabulous?
Actually, who are we not to be?
You are a child of the universe...
Your playing small doesn't serve the world.
There is nothing enlightening about shrinking so that others won't feel insecure around you,
We are all meant to shine, as children do,
We are born to manifest the glory of God that is within us.
It is not just in some of us; it is in everyone.
And as we let our own light shine, we unconsciously give other people permission to do the same.
As we're liberated from our fears, our presence automatically liberates each other.

**Marianne Williamson** (From her book "A Return to Love")

# WORDS OF INSPIRATION 3

*A friend once sent me a beautiful, hand-written card a few years ago – I refer to this card anytime I seek added inspiration.*

## Whatever You Can Do, or Dream you Can, Begin it

Until one is committed there is hesitancy, the chance to draw back, always ineffectiveness.

Concerning all acts of initiative there is one elementary truth, the ignorance of which kills countless ideas and endless plans.

That the moment one definitely commits oneself then providence moves too.

All sorts of things occur to help one that would never have otherwise occurred.

A whole stream of events issue from the decision, raising in one's favour all manner of unforeseen incidents, and meetings and material assistance which no man could have dreamed would come his way.

Whatever you can do, or dream you can, begin it. Boldness has genius, power, and magic in it.

Begin it now.

**Johann Wolfgang von Goethe**

# WORDS OF INSPIRATION 4

*I first came across these words when my younger sister gave me a beautiful card she had especially made for me.*

## Just for Today

Just for today I will try to live through this day only, and not tackle my whole life problem at once. I can do something for twelve hours that would appal me if I felt that I had to keep it up for a lifetime.

Just for today I will be happy. Most folk are as happy as they make up their minds to be.

Just for today I will adjust myself to what is, and not try to adjust everything to my own desires. I will take my 'luck' as it comes, and fit myself to it.

Just for today I will try to strengthen my mind. I will study. I will learn something useful. I will not be a mental loafer. I will read something that requires effort, thought and concentration.

Just for today I will exercise my soul in three ways:

- **I will do someone a good turn, and not get found out; if anybody knows of it, I will not count.**
- **I will do at least two things I don't want to do just for exercise.**
- **I will not show anyone that my feelings are hurt; they may be hurt, but today I will not show it.**

Just for today I will be agreeable. I will look as well as I can, dress becomingly, talk low, act courteously, criticise not one bit, not find fault with anything and not try to improve or regulate anybody except myself.

Just for today I will have a programme. I may not follow it exactly, but I will have it. I will save myself from two pests: hurry and indecision.

Just for today I will have a quiet half hour all by myself, and relax. During this half hour, sometime, I will try to get a better perspective of my life.

Just for today I will be unafraid. Especially I will not be afraid to enjoy what is beautiful, and to believe that as I give to the world, the world will give to me.

**Frank Crane**

*These words continue to remind me to make the most of myself and to live one day at a time.*

## One Day at a Time...

There are two days in every week about which we should not worry, two days which should be kept free from fear and apprehension.

One of these days is Yesterday with its mistakes and cares, its faults and blunders, its aches and pains. Yesterday has passed forever beyond our control.

All the money in the world cannot bring back Yesterday. We cannot undo a single act we performed; we cannot erase a single word said. Yesterday is gone.

The other day we should not worry about is Tomorrow with its possible adversities, its burdens, its large promise, and poor performance. Tomorrow is also beyond our immediate control.

Tomorrow's sun will rise, either in splendour or behind a mask of clouds - but it will rise. Until it does, we have no stake in Tomorrow, for it is yet unborn.

This leaves only one day - Today.

Any man can fight the battles of just one day; it is only when you or I add the burdens of those two awful eternities - Yesterday -and Tomorrow - that we break down.

It is not the experience of Today that drives men mad - it is the remorse or bitterness for something which happened Yesterday and the dread of what Tomorrow may bring.

Let us, therefore, live but One Day at a Time.

**Author unknown**

# WORDS OF INSPIRATION 6

*Originally written by Dr. Kent Keith, a version of these inspirational words were also found on a wall in Mother Teresa's children's home in Calcutta.*

## Plan for Life

People are illogical, unreasonable, and self-centred.
Love them anyway.

If you do good, people will accuse you of selfish ulterior motives.
Do good anyway.

If you are successful, you will win false friends and true enemies.
Succeed anyway.

The good you do today will be forgotten tomorrow.
Do good anyway.

Honesty and frankness make you vulnerable.
Be honest and frank anyway.

The biggest men and women with the biggest ideas can be shot down by the smallest men and women with the smallest minds.
Think big anyway.

People favour underdogs but follow only top dogs.
Fight for a few underdogs anyway.

What you spend years building may be destroyed overnight.
Build anyway.

People really need help but may attack you if you do help them.
Help people anyway.

Give the world the best you have, and you'll get kicked in the teeth.
Give the world the best you have anyway.

**Dr Kent Keith**

*I first came across Desiderata years ago during my college days. Recently a friend visiting from Ireland gave me a beautiful golden frame with these words etched on a collage of handmade papers and natural pressed flowers – one of the most beautiful gifts I have ever received and one to be treasured always.*

## Desiderata

Go placidly amid the noise and haste,
and remember what peace there may be in silence.
As far as possible without surrender
be on good terms with all persons.
Speak your truth quietly and clearly;
and listen to others,
even the dull and the ignorant;
they too have their story.

Avoid loud and aggressive persons,
they are vexations to the spirit.
If you compare yourself with others,
you may become vain and bitter;
for always there will be greater and lesser persons than yourself.
Enjoy your achievements as well as your plans.

Keep interested in your own career, however humble;
it is a real possession in the changing fortunes of time.
Exercise caution in your business affairs;
for the world is full of trickery.
But let this not blind you to what virtue there is;
many persons strive for high ideals;
and everywhere life is full of heroism.

Be yourself.
Especially, do not feign affection.
Neither be cynical about love;
for in the face of all aridity and disenchantment
it is as perennial as the grass.

Take kindly the counsel of the years,
gracefully surrendering the things of youth.
Nurture strength of spirit to shield you in sudden misfortune.
But do not distress yourself with dark imaginings.
Many fears are born of fatigue and loneliness.
Beyond a wholesome discipline,
be gentle with yourself.

You are a child of the universe,
no less than the trees and the stars;
you have a right to be here.
And whether or not it is clear to you,
no doubt the universe is unfolding as it should.

Therefore be at peace with God,
whatever you conceive Him to be,
and whatever your labours and aspirations,
in the noisy confusion of life keep peace with your soul.

With all its sham, drudgery, and broken dreams,
it is still a beautiful world.
Be cheerful.
Strive to be happy.

**Max Ehrmann**

# INSPIRING QUOTATIONS

| have included here my favourite quotations which will help you reflect and be inspired.

*Do what you love. Do what makes your heart sing. And never do it for the money. Don't go to work to make money, go to work to spread joy. Seek ye first the kingdom of Heaven, and the Maserati will get here when it is supposed to.* - **Marianne Williamson**

---

*I have missed more than 9,000 shots, lost almost 300 games, on 26 occasions been entrusted to take the game-winning shot... and missed. I have failed over and over again in my life. And that is why I succeeded.* - **Michael Jordan**

---

*If you want happiness for an hour — take a nap.*
*If you want happiness for a day — go fishing.*
*If you want happiness for a year — inherit a fortune.*
*If you want happiness for a lifetime — help someone else.* - **Chinese proverb**

---

*A choice for love creates love. A choice for fear creates fear. What choice do you think has been made to create the world you call your home? This world was created by your choice, and a new world can be created by a new choice. But you must realize that this is all there is. Love or lack of love. Love is all that is real.* - **Mari Perron**

---

*Kindness in words creates confidence.*
*Kindness in thinking creates profoundness.*
*Kindness in feeling creates love.* - **Lao-Tzu**

---

*I expect to pass through this world but once. Any good therefore that I can do, or any kindness that I can show to a fellow creature, let me do it now. Let me not defer or neglect it, for I shall not pass this way again.* - **William Penn**

---

*I believe life is constantly testing us for our level of commitment, and life's greatest rewards are reserved for those who demonstrate a never-ending commitment to act until they achieve. This level of resolve can move mountains, but it must be constant and consistent. As simplistic as this may sound, it is still the common denominator separating those who live their dreams from those who live in regret.* - **Anthony Robbins**

---

*What is Success?*

*To laugh often and much;*
*To win the respect of intelligent people and the affection of children;*
*To earn the appreciation of honest critics and endure the betrayal of false friends;*
*To appreciate beauty;*
*To find the best in others;*
*To leave the world a bit better, whether by a healthy child, a garden patch or a redeemed*
*social condition;*
*To know that even one life has breathed easier because you have lived; this is to have*
*succeeded.*

\- **Ralph Waldo Emerson**

---

*This is the true joy in life, the being used for a purpose recognised by yourself as a mighty*
*one; the being a force of nature instead of a feverish selfish little clod of ailments and griev-*
*ances complaining that the world will not devote itself to making you happy.*

*I am of the opinion that my life belongs to the whole community and as long as I live it is my*
*privilege to do for it whatever I can.*

*I want to be thoroughly used up when I die, for the harder I work the more I live. I rejoice*
*in life for its own sake.*

*Life is no 'Brief Candle' to me. It is a sort of splendid torch which I have got hold of for the*
*moment and I want to make it burn as brightly as possible before handling it on to future*
*generations.*

\- **George Bernard Shaw**

---

*I don't know what your destiny will be, but one thing I do know: the only ones among*
*you who will be really happy are those who have sought and found how to serve.* - **Albert**
**Schweitzer**

---

*If you have built castles in the air, your work need not be lost; that is where they should be.*
*Now put the foundations under them.* - **Henry David Thoreau**

---

*The love you fail to share is the only pain you live with right now in your life.* - **Shore Slocum**

---

*I think it's possible for ordinary people to choose to be extraordinary.* - **Elon Musk**

---

# NOTES - 1

Write here your insights from your transformational journey so far

. . . . . . . . . . . . . . . . . . . . . . . . . . . . . . . . . . . . . . . . . . . . . . . . . . .
. . . . . . . . . . . . . . . . . . . . . . . . . . . . . . . . . . . . . . . . . . . . . . . . . . .
. . . . . . . . . . . . . . . . . . . . . . . . . . . . . . . . . . . . . . . . . . . . . . . . . . .
. . . . . . . . . . . . . . . . . . . . . . . . . . . . . . . . . . . . . . . . . . . . . . . . . . .
. . . . . . . . . . . . . . . . . . . . . . . . . . . . . . . . . . . . . . . . . . . . . . . . . . .
. . . . . . . . . . . . . . . . . . . . . . . . . . . . . . . . . . . . . . . . . . . . . . . . . . .
. . . . . . . . . . . . . . . . . . . . . . . . . . . . . . . . . . . . . . . . . . . . . . . . . . .
. . . . . . . . . . . . . . . . . . . . . . . . . . . . . . . . . . . . . . . . . . . . . . . . . . .
. . . . . . . . . . . . . . . . . . . . . . . . . . . . . . . . . . . . . . . . . . . . . . . . . . .
. . . . . . . . . . . . . . . . . . . . . . . . . . . . . . . . . . . . . . . . . . . . . . . . . . .
. . . . . . . . . . . . . . . . . . . . . . . . . . . . . . . . . . . . . . . . . . . . . . . . . . .
. . . . . . . . . . . . . . . . . . . . . . . . . . . . . . . . . . . . . . . . . . . . . . . . . . .
. . . . . . . . . . . . . . . . . . . . . . . . . . . . . . . . . . . . . . . . . . . . . . . . . . .
. . . . . . . . . . . . . . . . . . . . . . . . . . . . . . . . . . . . . . . . . . . . . . . . . . .
. . . . . . . . . . . . . . . . . . . . . . . . . . . . . . . . . . . . . . . . . . . . . . . . . . .
. . . . . . . . . . . . . . . . . . . . . . . . . . . . . . . . . . . . . . . . . . . . . . . . . . .
. . . . . . . . . . . . . . . . . . . . . . . . . . . . . . . . . . . . . . . . . . . . . . . . . . .
. . . . . . . . . . . . . . . . . . . . . . . . . . . . . . . . . . . . . . . . . . . . . . . . . . .
. . . . . . . . . . . . . . . . . . . . . . . . . . . . . . . . . . . . . . . . . . . . . . . . . . .
. . . . . . . . . . . . . . . . . . . . . . . . . . . . . . . . . . . . . . . . . . . . . . . . . . .
. . . . . . . . . . . . . . . . . . . . . . . . . . . . . . . . . . . . . . . . . . . . . . . . . . .
. . . . . . . . . . . . . . . . . . . . . . . . . . . . . . . . . . . . . . . . . . . . . . . . . . .
. . . . . . . . . . . . . . . . . . . . . . . . . . . . . . . . . . . . . . . . . . . . . . . . . . .
. . . . . . . . . . . . . . . . . . . . . . . . . . . . . . . . . . . . . . . . . . . . . . . . . . .
. . . . . . . . . . . . . . . . . . . . . . . . . . . . . . . . . . . . . . . . . . . . . . . . . . .

# NOTES - 2

Write here your insights from your transformational journey so far.

. . . . . . . . . . . . . . . . . . . . . . . . . . . . . . . . . . . . . . . . . . . . . . . . . . . .
. . . . . . . . . . . . . . . . . . . . . . . . . . . . . . . . . . . . . . . . . . . . . . . . . . . .
. . . . . . . . . . . . . . . . . . . . . . . . . . . . . . . . . . . . . . . . . . . . . . . . . . . .
. . . . . . . . . . . . . . . . . . . . . . . . . . . . . . . . . . . . . . . . . . . . . . . . . . . .
. . . . . . . . . . . . . . . . . . . . . . . . . . . . . . . . . . . . . . . . . . . . . . . . . . . .
. . . . . . . . . . . . . . . . . . . . . . . . . . . . . . . . . . . . . . . . . . . . . . . . . . . .
. . . . . . . . . . . . . . . . . . . . . . . . . . . . . . . . . . . . . . . . . . . . . . . . . . . .
. . . . . . . . . . . . . . . . . . . . . . . . . . . . . . . . . . . . . . . . . . . . . . . . . . . .
. . . . . . . . . . . . . . . . . . . . . . . . . . . . . . . . . . . . . . . . . . . . . . . . . . . .
. . . . . . . . . . . . . . . . . . . . . . . . . . . . . . . . . . . . . . . . . . . . . . . . . . . .
. . . . . . . . . . . . . . . . . . . . . . . . . . . . . . . . . . . . . . . . . . . . . . . . . . . .
. . . . . . . . . . . . . . . . . . . . . . . . . . . . . . . . . . . . . . . . . . . . . . . . . . . .
. . . . . . . . . . . . . . . . . . . . . . . . . . . . . . . . . . . . . . . . . . . . . . . . . . . .
. . . . . . . . . . . . . . . . . . . . . . . . . . . . . . . . . . . . . . . . . . . . . . . . . . . .
. . . . . . . . . . . . . . . . . . . . . . . . . . . . . . . . . . . . . . . . . . . . . . . . . . . .
. . . . . . . . . . . . . . . . . . . . . . . . . . . . . . . . . . . . . . . . . . . . . . . . . . . .
. . . . . . . . . . . . . . . . . . . . . . . . . . . . . . . . . . . . . . . . . . . . . . . . . . . .
. . . . . . . . . . . . . . . . . . . . . . . . . . . . . . . . . . . . . . . . . . . . . . . . . . . .
. . . . . . . . . . . . . . . . . . . . . . . . . . . . . . . . . . . . . . . . . . . . . . . . . . . .
. . . . . . . . . . . . . . . . . . . . . . . . . . . . . . . . . . . . . . . . . . . . . . . . . . . .
. . . . . . . . . . . . . . . . . . . . . . . . . . . . . . . . . . . . . . . . . . . . . . . . . . . .
. . . . . . . . . . . . . . . . . . . . . . . . . . . . . . . . . . . . . . . . . . . . . . . . . . . .
. . . . . . . . . . . . . . . . . . . . . . . . . . . . . . . . . . . . . . . . . . . . . . . . . . . .
. . . . . . . . . . . . . . . . . . . . . . . . . . . . . . . . . . . . . . . . . . . . . . . . . . . .

# NOTES - 3

Write here your insights from your transformational journey so far.

. . . . . . . . . . . . . . . . . . . . . . . . . . . . . . . . . . . . . . . . . .
. . . . . . . . . . . . . . . . . . . . . . . . . . . . . . . . . . . . . . . . . .
. . . . . . . . . . . . . . . . . . . . . . . . . . . . . . . . . . . . . . . . . .
. . . . . . . . . . . . . . . . . . . . . . . . . . . . . . . . . . . . . . . . . .
. . . . . . . . . . . . . . . . . . . . . . . . . . . . . . . . . . . . . . . . . .
. . . . . . . . . . . . . . . . . . . . . . . . . . . . . . . . . . . . . . . . . .
. . . . . . . . . . . . . . . . . . . . . . . . . . . . . . . . . . . . . . . . . .
. . . . . . . . . . . . . . . . . . . . . . . . . . . . . . . . . . . . . . . . . .
. . . . . . . . . . . . . . . . . . . . . . . . . . . . . . . . . . . . . . . . . .
. . . . . . . . . . . . . . . . . . . . . . . . . . . . . . . . . . . . . . . . . .
. . . . . . . . . . . . . . . . . . . . . . . . . . . . . . . . . . . . . . . . . .
. . . . . . . . . . . . . . . . . . . . . . . . . . . . . . . . . . . . . . . . . .
. . . . . . . . . . . . . . . . . . . . . . . . . . . . . . . . . . . . . . . . . .
. . . . . . . . . . . . . . . . . . . . . . . . . . . . . . . . . . . . . . . . . .
. . . . . . . . . . . . . . . . . . . . . . . . . . . . . . . . . . . . . . . . . .
. . . . . . . . . . . . . . . . . . . . . . . . . . . . . . . . . . . . . . . . . .
. . . . . . . . . . . . . . . . . . . . . . . . . . . . . . . . . . . . . . . . . .
. . . . . . . . . . . . . . . . . . . . . . . . . . . . . . . . . . . . . . . . . .
. . . . . . . . . . . . . . . . . . . . . . . . . . . . . . . . . . . . . . . . . .
. . . . . . . . . . . . . . . . . . . . . . . . . . . . . . . . . . . . . . . . . .
. . . . . . . . . . . . . . . . . . . . . . . . . . . . . . . . . . . . . . . . . .
. . . . . . . . . . . . . . . . . . . . . . . . . . . . . . . . . . . . . . . . . .
. . . . . . . . . . . . . . . . . . . . . . . . . . . . . . . . . . . . . . . . . .

# RECOMMENDED BOOKS

These are some of the books I have found useful during my journey of growth and transformation, and which I recommend to my coaching clients. I invite you to also check these out for your own journey:-

*A Return to Love* – Marianne Williamson

*The Alchemist* – Paulo Coelho

*You Can Heal Your Life* – Louise Hay

*The Four Agreements* – Don Miguel Ruiz

*The Mastery of Love* – Don Miguel Ruiz

*Inner Engineering* – Sadhguru

*Straight Line Leadership* – Dusan Djukich

*The Art of Possibility* – Rosamund Stone Zander

*The Seven Spiritual Laws of Success* – Deepak Chopra

*The Universe has your back* – Gabby Bernstein

*Loving What Is* – Byron Katie

*Turning Pro* – Steven Pressfield

*The Monk Who Sold His Ferrari* – Robin Sharma

*The Life-Changing Magic of Tidying* – Marie Kondo

*The Ultimate Coach* – Amy Hardison & Alan D. Thompson

*Atomic Habits* – James Clear

*Breaking the Habit of Being Yourself* – Dr Joe Dispenza

*Creative Visualization* – Shakti Gawain

*Time Warrior* – Steve Chandler

*Daring Greatly* – Brene Brown

*Loveability – Knowing How to Love and Be Loved* – Robert Holden

*Money and the Law of Attraction* – Esther & Abraham Hicks

*The Code of the Extraordinary Mind* – Vishen Lakhiani

*The Go–Giver* – Bob Burg & John David Mann

*The Seven Habits of Highly Effective People* – Steven R Covey

*Way of the Peaceful Warrior* – Dan Millman

*Jonathan Livingstone Seagull* – Richard Bach

## WITH DEEP GRATITUDE

**I would like to thank firstly you, for wanting to take on your life and to make it the best possible. Always remember that your life is a gift.**

I thank my late parents, family, friends and clients for your support, encouragement, humour and most importantly your love.

I thank all those kind, generous and talented people who have made this book possible and allowed me to fulfil my dream of being a best-selling author.

A heartfelt thanks to my best friend who has inspired me even more to be the best I can be. Thank you for your deep love and special friendship. Please always be you and continue to be open to all possibilities.

Thank you all for allowing me to be me.

Thank you all for being you.

**I am deeply grateful to you all.**

# FURTHER KEY RESOURCES

Continue your life adventure and journey of growth with Arvind via www.ArvindDevalia.com

- Transform your life with deep powerful coaching - one to one or in a group programme.
- Join a 12-week programme to support you, as you go through this book.
- Receive regular newsletters delivered to your email box - packed with powerful ideas and smart tips to help you get the most out of your life.
- Read over 500 life-changing articles.
- Follow Social Media posts for daily inspiration.
- Sign up for workshops, inspirational talks, and events, where you can transform your life and meet other like-minded people.

**Final message from Arvind:-**

You can be so much more than you believe.

Let's continue together your onward journey of deep transformation. When you transform, the world transforms too.

Join me in transforming the world.

Get in touch and let me know how I can serve you.

Thank you.
Arvind
www.ArvindDevalia.com

# ABOUT THE AUTHOR

**A**rvind Devalia is passionate about people and is committed to living an extraordinary life of contribution, connection, and celebration.

He strives to live a life of service and his vision is to help as many people as possible in being the best they can be, to connect them with their true passion, and to ultimately create a joy-filled life they love, by inspiring and supporting them as a friend, coach, mentor, writer, and speaker.

Though Arvind has spent many years on his own growth and development and studied the teachings of some of the world's greatest teachers, he is very much a work in progress with his own life challenges and growth opportunities. He is learning and growing every day and considers himself to be deeply blessed to be able to continue to learn, grown and play full out.

Having worked with hundreds of coaching clients, Arvind has distilled his learnings into this powerful coaching playbook which will transform your life in just 12 weeks. You just have to take the deceptively simple but powerful actions outlined here and your life will magically transform.

Arvind believes that there is something special and unique about every human being.

**Your fondest dreams can come true, and everyone has the capacity to realise them.**

"Life is meant to be simple, but we complicate it," he says. "Life is meant to be a joy in all areas of your life – you can live and enjoy each day as you wish".

"You can all get the life you love – and live it."

"And remember that ultimately, Love is all that matters".

Arvind lives in St John's Wood, central London, from where he runs his coaching practice and is available for private consultation in person or online.

To connect with Arvind and for more information about his coaching programmes, and his current world changing activities and projects, please visit:-

www.ArvindDevalia.com

Made in the USA
Middletown, DE
09 March 2023

26409174R00076